Rebirth Brass Band   *Photo by John McCusker. Courtesy Hogan Jazz Archive, Tulane University.*

Majestic Brass Band (Joe Taylor, Jerome Davis, Flo Anckle) *Photo by Marcel Joly*

The people got the soul. We don't have it. They always say, "The band got the soul."
We don't have no soul. The people got the soul.

—FLOYD "FLO" ANCKLE, leader, Majestic Brass Band

KEEPING THE BEAT
ON THE STREET

The New Orleans

Brass Band Renaissance

MICK BURNS

LOUISIANA STATE UNIVERSITY PRESS

BATON ROUGE

Published by Louisiana State University Press

Manufactured in the United States of America
SECOND PRINTING, 2006

DESIGNER: Andrew Shurtz
TYPEFACE: Tribute
PRINTER AND BINDER: Edwards Brothers, Inc.

LIBRARY OF CONGRESS CATALOGING-IN-PUBLICATION DATA

Burns, Mick, 1942–
    Keeping the beat on the street : the New Orleans brass band renaissance / Mick Burns.
        p.   cm.
    Includes bibliographical references (p.   ), discography (p.   ), and index.
    ISBN 0-8071-3048-6 (cloth : alk. paper)
    1. Bands (Music)—Louisiana—New Orleans.   2. Jazz—Louisiana—New Orleans—History
and criticism.   3. Musicians—Louisiana—New Orleans.   4. New Orleans (La.)—Social life
and customs.   I. Title.
ML1311.8.N48B87 2005
784.9′165′0976335—dc22

Published with support from the Louisiana Sea Grant College Program, a part of the National
Sea Grant College program maintained by the National Oceanic and Atmospheric Administra-
tion of the U.S. Department of Commerce.

To the memory of Anthony "Tuba Fats" Lacen

Contents

Illustrations

Acknowledgments

Thanks and acknowledgments are due to

The Board of Directors of the New Orleans Jazz and Heritage Foundation, Executive Director Wali Abdel Ra'oof, Program Director Sharon Martin, and Archivist Rachel Lyons, for their support and contributions

The Lincolnshire County Council

Jazzology Press, for permission to reprint passages from my book *The Great Olympia Band*

New Orleans Music, for permission to reprint "Anthony Lacen: Goodbye Tuba Fats"

The New Orleans Jazz Commission and the New Orleans Jazz National Historical Park

The William Ransom Hogan Jazz Archive at Tulane University, Curator Bruce Boyd Raeburn, and Lynn Abbott and Alma Williams Freeman

The Amistad Research Center at Tulane University, Director of Archives Brenda Square, and Heidi Dodson

Parker Dinkins, Peter Nissen, Brian Wood, Bill Bissonette, Emile Martyn, Anthony Lacen, and Helen Regis

Marcel Joly, Bill Dickens, Butch Gomez, Mike Casimir, Leroy Jones, Dave Cirilli, and Mike Peters, who provided photographs

Holly Hardiman, who helped with the index

The musicians and citizens of New Orleans, who gave freely of their time for interviews so that this story could be told

Barry Martyn, whose assistance was invaluable

Louisiana State University Press and editor George Roupe

KEEPING THE BEAT ON THE STREET

Introduction

The early years of the twentieth century saw the explosive beginnings of the most culturally significant American art form, jazz. The influence of this creative phenomenon born in New Orleans changed things for ever. The whole spectrum of music, from Tin Pan Alley to musical shows to Stravinsky and Shostakovich, reflected the spirit and sound that first found expression on the streets of a city in southern Louisiana. Louis Armstrong, Sidney Bechet, Kid Ory, and King Oliver achieved considerable personal success outside the city. But they were the most visible members of a larger diaspora that carried the new music not only across America but to London, Paris, Cairo, Moscow, and Beijing. Almost all the practitioners of this new art form found a cradle for their burgeoning talents in the brass bands, which had been around for decades before jazz began. One hundred and thirty years later, the brass bands of New Orleans still perform the same function they always did and still provide a crucible for the seemingly inexhaustible supply of creative fire that is New Orleans music.

According to contemporary accounts, the first black brass bands in New Orleans appear to have hit the streets in the 1870s. Typically consisting of nine or ten pieces, they played whatever they could get hired to play—dignified sonorous dirges for funerals, sprightly military marches for parades, and popular hits of the day for dances and concerts. At that time, the brass band movement, mostly fueled by amateur musicians, flourished all over America and Europe—there were bands attached to villages, churches, factories, plantations, and coal mines; they served as a creative outlet for the working man and a symbol of celebration and solidarity for their communities.

In the beginning, there probably wasn't much difference between a brass band in New Orleans and, for example, northern England—"Shepherd of the Hills" played competently from a written score is going to sound very similar wherever it happens. What makes New Orleans brass band music unique is the way the musicians started with the same ingredients as everyone else and transformed them into a vital art form. Today, a brass band in New Orleans will kick off on a bass lick, play a continuous collective improvisation (no written music) and keep it going for as long as forty minutes. In northern England, the brass bands are still reading "Shepherd of the Hills."

How did this happen? In the absence of recordings, we have to rely on contemporary accounts for the start of the process. According to Richard Knowles's excellent book *Fallen Heroes* (Jazzology Press) the emerging "hot" style of playing first appeared in a brass band context with the Tuxedo Brass Band, under the leadership of trumpet player Oscar Celestin, sometime after 1910.

Celestin also led a hugely popular dance band, and many of the city's top players (including some early jazz legends) worked for both organizations. We can only speculate on the extent to which improvisation and swing appeared on the street in those early days, although King Oliver's 1923 recording of the march "High Society" offers a broad hint.

In 1929, a film newsreel soundtrack captured the first recorded sound of a New Orleans brass band playing at a Mardi Gras parade. Although there's only a brief snatch of muffled music, a unique Crescent City characteristic can clearly be heard—the seductive, propulsive rhythmic device called the "second line beat."

In simple terms, this describes a syncopated pattern on the bass drum that may be phonetically rendered as "Dah, Dah, Dah, Didit, Da!" Transfer this rhythmic feel to the horns, and the whole band swings—it makes you want to dance. Of course, there were many bands who could play both written music for formal events and, for want of a better word, improvised "swing" for the dancing crowd. Bands that couldn't, or didn't, read music, were dismissively called "tonk" bands by more formally inclined musicians. But it was the ability and inclination to depart from the written score that made New Orleans brass bands so special. In a sense, you could describe the whole creative evolution of brass band music as the triumph of "tonk."

Over the next couple of decades, there were other stylistic changes—the rich, chorale-like scoring of formal funeral dirges gave way to the simpler harmonies of Baptist hymns, apparently in response to popular preference. The function of supplying the inner harmonies (the parts between the melody and the bass line) was originally allocated to the tenor and baritone horns, familiarly known as "peck horns." By the 1940s, there was a collective tendency to replace them with saxophones. They probably made a band sound less resonant when playing written music, but they were more musically suited to the rhythmic and improvisational demands of playing "hot." By the middle of the 1960s, many of the musicians in the brass bands worked nights in rhythm and blues bands, and this also changed the repertoire and the way it was played.

In the face of so much change, what do we mean by "tradition" in New Orleans brass band music? Ask any working musician in New Orleans today, and the probable response will be a tune list—something like "Oh yeah, man, we stick to the tradition. We play like 'Just a Closer Walk,' 'Bye Bye Blackbird,' 'Second Line,' that kind of thing." Trumpet player William Smith added the proviso "But don't expect the phrasing to be the same. It's not that clear cut."[1] Indeed it isn't. Irrespective of the material, the manner of performance reflects the contemporary nature of the musicians, and it always has. This is a living art form, not an exercise in preservation.

A member of Dejan's Olympia Brass Band (for many years, the number one brass band in the city) told me a story about working uptown for a neighborhood function. Milton Batiste, the trumpet player, had opened the evening by calling a play list of old songs—"Over in Gloryland," "Panama," and "Just a Little While to Stay Here." Nobody danced until the disco started up, and then the man paid the band off and sent them home without playing their second set. "We should have played our rhythm and blues things for those people," said my friend. "That traditional stuff, that's white folks' music."

This is a bit of an oversimplification. "White folks and old folks" would be nearer the mark. People don't always know what they like, but they definitely like what they know. The older generation are obviously more comfortable with the music they grew up with, and white conventioneers, when they have any expectations at all, want to hear something that approximates Dixieland music. So white folks and old folks both prefer listening to those old tunes, but their way of participating in the music is quite different.

I was privileged to play at a funeral at St. Michael's church on Gentilly Boulevard in the mid 1990s. The band was Tuba Fats's Chosen Few, consisting of Anthony "Tuba Fats" Lacen (tuba), Mervyn Campbell (trumpet), Mick Burns (trombone), Frederick Shepherd and Ernest Watson (saxophones), Benny Jones (snare drum), and Lionel Batiste Sr. (bass drum). At the request of the family, the repertoire was drawn from the old Baptist hymnbook, the band wore uniforms and parade caps, played with great reverence and restraint, and marched (and slow marched) in formal ranks. Everyone knew why we were there, we all had our roles to play, and the whole event had a sense of purpose and completeness, the music and the grief feeding off each other in the morning sunshine. A few days later, a lady stopped me on the sidewalk on Decatur Street. "Excuse me, sir," she said. "I just wanted to say thank you for playing so beautifully at my uncle's funeral on Monday."

A few years later, I was lucky enough to pick up a job at the convention center with Andrew Hall's Society Brass Band. The band consisted of Barry Martyn (bass drum), Emile Martyn (snare drum), Wendell Eugene (trombone), Mick Burns (tuba), Chris Clifton (trumpet), and Joe Torregano (saxophone). Again, the band wore uniforms, and the repertoire was drawn from the old-time bag—"Fidgety Feet," "Lord, Lord, Lord," and so forth. It was the audience that was different.

At 5:00 P.M., the doors to one of the lecture theaters opened, and hundreds of delegates poured out, wearing Mardi Gras beads in November. One minute they'd been listening to next year's marketing strategy or, even worse, an "inspirational address," and within seconds, they were getting "Just a Little While to Stay Here" from a distance of less than twenty feet. Initial expressions of shock gave way to embarrassed grins (obviously, this was meant to be fun!) and off we all went for a "parade." What we actually did was march round the narrow aisles of the exhibition hall (the sousaphone bell demolishing various overhanging signs), trailed by a very long crowd—three people abreast is the most those aisles can take. Then it was out of the building and over the street to a seemingly endless rendition of "When the Saints" while our audience clambered on to buses—the embarrassed grins had by now acquired a discernibly frozen quality. As far as the band was concerned, that was the end of the job, and the buses whisked the delegates away, to be force-fed their next "New Orleans" experience.

Both the funeral and the convention center jobs are part of a working brass band musician's routine, and both jobs paid about the same. In both cases, the bands played similar music. The crucial difference seems to me to be between the dignified ritual on Gentilly Boulevard, in which the mourners were participants, and the manufactured quality of the convention center parade, where the crowd were mystified onlookers.

My point (at last!) is that the synergy between the band and the crowd is a more significant part of the brass band tradition than the style of music being played.

Currently, there are probably more brass bands active in New Orleans than ever before. Exactly how many is uncertain, but twenty-five bands seems a reasonable estimate, and there are probably around a hundred and fifty musicians involved. Some bands' personnel is more or less constant, but for others it's a question of availability and budget, and the musicians change from job to job. New bands are being formed all the time, and the scene is constantly changing.

This book is not intended to be a fully comprehensive survey, and the way things are, I don't think that would be possible. There are no interviews here with the Hot 8, the Soul Rebels, or the Lil' Rascals, and there are many others that I didn't get around to. What I have tried to do is to trace major developments in the music over the last thirty years, and interview some of the key players. The information contained in the interviews records the musical evolution of the brass bands and the social and commercial pressures that caused these changes.

This isn't a music invented by record companies or marketing departments; it's one that grows on the streets, supported by the neighborhoods. The primary demand for brass bands is the second line parades and funerals held by the hugely expanded social and pleasure club network. Louis Armstrong's recollections of the early twenties in New Orleans are an indication of how far back the tradition goes:

> The Second Line is a bunch of Guys who follows the parade. They're not the members of the Lodge or the Club. Anybody can be a Second Liner, whether they are Raggedy or dressed up. They seemed to have more fun than anybody. (They will start a free-for-all fight any minute—with broom handles, baseball bats, pistols, knives, razors, brickbats, etc.) The Onward Brass Band, Broke up a Baseball game, over in Algiers, La., when they passed by the game playing—"When the Saints Go Marching In." The Game Stopped immediately and followed the parade.[2]

These clubs parade one Sunday per year (usually on the club's anniversary) and always hire a brass band for the parade, sometimes as many as three. In the early seventies, the club parade season ran from September to November; nowadays, there are parades most Sundays from September until May. There are well over sixty social and pleasure clubs currently active, and they create a steady grass roots demand for brass band musicians.

Where does this pool of talent come from? Up until relatively recently, straight brass bands—playing Sousa marches and marching in formation—were a feature of most public schools in the city. Prior to 1970, what few New Orleans brass bands there were consisted mainly of veteran musicians, who didn't work that often. The tendency among younger players was to regard these bands as relics of the past and, in the social climate following the civil rights movement, as having "Uncle Tom" connotations. There were *some* younger musicians working with the uptown nonunion bands like the E. Gibson Band, Doc Paulin, and Big Nat Dowe—Eddie King, Anthony Lacen, Gregg Stafford, and Albert Miller spring to mind—but there were not more than a handful of young musicians then. At that time, there were relatively few clubs, and not many bands either. The whole neighborhood parade scene was more or less moribund, and most people saw it as increasingly old fashioned and irrelevant.

Doc Paulin's band was operational under his leadership until just a few years ago, and he always encouraged younger talent by taking them into his band, providing on-the-job training. Individual musicians like Clarence Ford and Nat Dowe held impromptu lessons for aspiring youngsters on their front porches. Milton Batiste created and coached three different versions of the Junior Olympia band during the eighties, based largely on the Tambourine and Fan Club (a neighborhood youth sports and social club). And in a less direct way, musicians were role models for neighborhood youngsters. "When I was a kid, I remember musicians always had the nicest shoes," recalls trumpet player William Smith. "They were sort of a bridge between the haves and have nots."[3]

The beginning of the movement toward contemporary younger brass bands was undoubtedly Danny Barker's Fairview Baptist Church Brass Band, started in 1971. It was this band that first made brass band music "cool" for a generation of young people and made it commercially viable to have a band consisting mostly of teenagers. Although both the Fairview band and the various Tambourine and Fan youth bands were formed primarily for social reasons—keeping the young-sters off the streets—their combined musical influence on the brass band renais-sance has been incalculable.

The first response of any New Orleans crowd to a brass band is to move—that is what the music is for. Dance fashions, and the music that makes them possible, change all the time, and this as much as anything had led to the perception of the old-style bands as out of date. By the mid-seventies, Dejan's Olympia Brass Band was reaching the crowds with rhythm and blues themes like "No It Ain't My Fault," "Mardi Gras in New Orleans" and "I Got a Woman." The Majestic Brass Band was doing "Majestic Stomp" (actually "Shake, Rattle, and Roll") and "Hey Pocky Way." The fledgling Hurricane Band had "Leroy Special" and several blues-based originals.

None of these bands had that much work on the sparse second line circuit, but they generated a collective style that came to brilliant fruition with the Dirty Dozen Brass Band. Despite the various members' modestly claiming that they didn't really do anything new, the Dirty Dozen changed the whole thing. Their first album (which the members of Rebirth Brass Band call their "bible") was titled *My Feet Can't Fail Me Now*, originally a catchphrase used by the great black dancer Bill "Bojangles" Robinson. The phrase had become a chant from the second line at Sunday parades, the band had made a song out of it, and it had become the anthem of the street. The distinctive thing about the title track is that, apart from a humorous run through the harmonies of "I Got Rhythm" a couple of times, the song has no chord changes—it's a series of staccato riffs over a fixed bass figure and against a busy pushing rhythm from the snare. It was the precursor of what is now called "funk," "street," "urban," or "simple" music by the musicians, who draw a distinction between "street" and "jazz" playing—the former has a much freer approach to harmony and relies extensively on "open" chords and blues scales from the horns. The faster urgency of modern dance rhythm is achieved by filling in the beat on both bass and snare drum and adding extra percussion in the form of cowbell and tambourine.

Many of the clubs prefer "street" for dancing to, claiming that it has more soul and feeling—play them something with chord changes, and they stop dancing. Crucial to setting the groove is the bass horn "hook" on which street playing is based.

Veteran tuba player Walter Payton, for many years the foundation of the Young Tuxedo Brass Band, recognized the skill of the younger players: "I think the young brass bass players are great," he told me. "I admire what they're doing, and I couldn't play with the Soul Rebels or the Rebirth without extensive rehearsals. I mean, they have arrangements, and those bass players, they're playing a part—they got a line that they're playing. I'd need a written line, that's the only way I could do it." But the older generation often felt less than comfortable with the new sounds. As Tremé businessman Norman Smith observed,

> The dirges were very distinctive—maybe that was a characteristic of the musicians who played them. There was not this jubilant attitude that we see now. Today we see many of the hymns played up tempo, and so you have masses of people who come around to dance to the hymns. We know that these are uninformed people who don't understand the real significance of what this is.
>
> The music today is distinctly different—it's a lot faster and brighter and sharper; it's a lot more rhythmic in terms of the street dancing today. Those old guys played a different type of music—it was deeply spiritual. It's changed a lot. But then, we're all living a little faster than we used to. Everything must change, and it sort of meets the needs of the time.[4]

There are bands who describe themselves as "strictly traditional," whose approach to both harmony and repertoire is more conservative, notably the Algiers Brass Band and the Mahogany Brass Band. However, neither of these bands, by their own admission, do much work for the social and pleasure clubs, and the Algiers band in particular seems to be gravitating toward the French Quarter, the convention center, and work overseas. The most successful of the contemporary musicians are able to play in both "traditional" and "funk" styles.

The rise of rap music and hip-hop; their infiltration into the New Orleans brass band scene; their prevailing ethos of materialism, instant gratification, and guns as fashion accessories; and the echo of these values in the social standards of the New Orleans neighborhoods often give rise to a regret for the loss of the past. Restaurateur Leah Chase explained, "We were religious, plain people, we were happy people, we were clean as whistles, we were starched and ironed; if we had moved on, but kept those things, we would be top of the heap of the black community."[5] As one resident told researcher Helen Regis, "We used to sleep outside at night in the screened porch. You can't do that anymore! Hmm. We didn't even have locks on our doors!"[6] Regis then observes, "Such behavior would be lunacy today. But the bodily sensation of a gentle cool breeze momentarily brought back the memory of past pleasures and with it a bitter sense of what the city's regime of terror has cost us."[7]

The rise in popularity of the new brass bands since 1980 has been paralleled, and perhaps helped, by a corresponding growth in local media exposure and an opening up of opportunities. Apart from the Sunday parades and funerals, the first level of opportunity was jobs in clubs and bars around the city. This gave rise to comment and features on the relatively new WWOZ radio station and regular publications like *OffBeat*. Prior to the eighties, New Orleans music attracted virtually no media coverage, but since the advent of media outlets such as these, bands can attain local celebrity status fairly easily. After all, music journalists have to write about something.

During the mid-seventies, Dejan's Olympia Brass Band had blazed a trail for others to follow, touring Europe, making local jukebox hits, doing prestigious out-of-town jobs in the U.S., and appearing in TV commercials and major feature movies. All of this had been unheard of before, but it opened things up for the bands that came later.

Today, all these opportunities are available to brass bands. Recording deals worth $250,000, nationwide TV documentaries—these are life-changing events. If you're in the right place at the right time, New Orleans brass band music can be very lucrative, if only for the lucky few. But for everybody in the brass bands, it starts (and rests) with the social and pleasure clubs and the second line.

Whether the revitalization of the brass bands gave rise to the increase in social and pleasure clubs or the other way round, I don't know, and I don't think it matters. In the 2002 parade season, there were forty-four parades scheduled,

Zulu Social Aid and Pleasure Club with Tremé Brass Band, 1990. *Photo by Bill Dickens*

often using three bands each—that's a lot of work, and that's without the funerals and outside jobs that the clubs generate.

Membership confers status and a sense of order. As Norman Smith explained, "People who participated in the clubs and the second lines were revered as individuals who were trying to maintain and preserve our culture. We were very poor, and there were too many mouths to feed for us to afford to participate in the clubs, but my family were very supportive of the participants. We had more second lines in the Tremé than anywhere else—we became a very traditional brass band–oriented community."[8] Helen Regis notes that the "clubs provide alternative role models for children coming up in the central city." She quotes Buck Jumpers founder Frank Charles as saying, "All they [children] see is dealers and pimps" in the inner city neighborhoods, but they learn that in the social and pleasure clubs "you can be somebody."[9]

What is often not appreciated is the considerable financial outlay involved for the social and pleasure club members. Brass bands cost around $1,500 for a four-hour parade (the duration of the city permit), a police escort costs $600, and individual club members sometimes spend as much as $1,000 on shoes alone. "At the same time that the city employs the iconic second line in its self-marketing," notes Regis, "it heavily taxes the social and pleasure clubs for their anniversary parades.

Jolly Bunch parade, 1973, second line and band
Photo by Bill Dickens

They are required to buy permits, insurance, and police protection, which, with the price of the brass band, cost several thousands of dollars, a significant amount to clubs whose members hold down two or three jobs to meet their expenses."[10] Nevertheless, many members "spend from five to six hundred dollars" dressing up for their parades, says Norman Dixon. "It's according to how you want to look. The more money you put into it, the better you're going to look, and this is what it's all about. Once a year, you spend the money for yourself. You avoid your family, just to have that one day. The family's behind you all the way."[11]

But the thousands of people making up the sixty or more clubs obviously feel that it's money well spent, just to feel the joyous energy of Sunday afternoons on the streets. As Walter Payton put it, "When you entertain the people, it bounces back, and you get that vibe, that electricity."

How do brass bands achieve success beyond the local recognition of the second line? Basically, there are three obvious ways to earn a living: club appearances, touring, and recording. Each of these working situations releases the band from a combination of restraints. They no longer have to work outdoors, they don't have to play acoustically, and they don't have to be mobile. There are huge differences between presenting a forty-minute stage set and playing for four hours to an alfresco crowd.

If most of your jobs are on a stage, then, like the Dirty Dozen's are, it's logical to use a regular drum set. Once you've done that, then why not have a guitar or keyboards? There's nothing new in this: the old Onward Brass Band did stage concerts with a banjo, and Dejan's Olympia regularly played club dates with a lineup that included piano and conventional drum set. So the sound itself changes, the presentation has to be tighter, and the music will have more emphasis on vocals, solos, and entertainment content.

The recently formed Forgotten Souls Brass Band was aimed specifically at recordings and concerts. They get their massive percussion sound by using both snare and bass drum *and* a conventional drum set. And at least a couple of other brass bands have been making local club dates with a deejay and turntables!

In the early 1990s, the Young Olympia Brass Band was formed under the aegis of Milton Batiste, led by trumpet player Mervyn Campbell. The band worked under two different names: it was the Young Olympia by day for what the band called "traditional" events, and by night they were the Soul Rebels, supplying "funky" music for nightclubs and parties. The Rebels came up with their own musical thing. Their first CD, *Let Your Mind Be Free,* features a combination of influences—rap, funk, reggae, and jazz—and many original compositions, lots of vocals, tight arrangements, and blistering New Orleans energy. They've had a lot of success with club audiences—they were resident at Donna's Bar and Grill for a long time, and the last time I checked, they were holding down weekly engagements at El Matador, Le Bon Temps Roulé, and Café Brazil. But the Rebels band was never intended to work on the street. How can you rap without a microphone to thousands of people? So the title of their latest CD, *No More Parades,* seems a bit redundant, particularly considering that the cover photograph features possibly the least street-friendly of instruments, the vibraphone.

Bands like this have found their own niche success, and they play serious music. I think it's fair to regard them as from the brass band movement, rather than of it—although you'll often find the individual members of these stage bands on the street on Sunday afternoons, working for Benny Jones in the Tremé Brass Band!

BAND CALL

Fairview Baptist Church Brass Band
Hurricane Brass Band
Chosen Few Brass Band

Danny Barker and the Fairview Baptist Church Brass Band

Danny Barker
Photo by Marcel Joly

"The Fairview Baptist Church is very crude and very small," observed one contributor to the Louisiana Writers Project's *Gumbo Ya-Ya*. "There is a stove to one side; the long wooden benches are painted a dull grey. On the pulpit were more wooden benches, a piano and a preacher."[12] When this description was written, the church stood in an area called Pailet Lane; there were no sewerage mains or street lighting, cows grazed among the uncut weeds, and work had only just started on the St. Bernard housing project. But by the time Danny Barker returned to New Orleans in 1965, the area immediately east of City Park had been considerably redeveloped, and the Fairview Baptist Church, by then a handsome and substantial building, stood at the end of a neat row of suburban houses on St. Denis Street. Pailet Lane seems to have disappeared from the New Orleans street directory.

Danny Barker, like so many other musicians, had left New Orleans and moved north to earn a living. He fashioned a long and illustrious career playing with, among others, Cab Calloway, Lucky Millinder, and Jelly Roll Morton. On return to the Crescent City, he moved back to the area near the Fairview Church.

In 1972, Fairview pastor Rev. Andrew Darby approached Danny to form a youth brass band affiliated with the church; the stated aim was to keep the youngsters off the streets. The idea of having youth bands attached to churches was not new in New Orleans: in 1921, saxophonist Emanuel Paul got his start, along with Sam Dutrey, in a band attached to the Broadway Baptist Church in Carrollton. But whereas the Broadway church band folded after only a few weeks, the Fairview band was to prove almost too successful for its own good. As Danny was quoted as saying in the 1980s,

When you give a kid a musical instrument, he does something with his personality. He becomes a figure, and he's not so apt to get into trouble. Later on, the kids got into grass and narcotics, but in those days, families would encourage you to play music. There was something about playing music that gave you something special. You are not a waster or a bum. Now you can be a musician and still be those things, but generally you were a little something special when you were a musician.[13]

He started the Fairview Baptist Church Band with the Reverend Darby and soon attracted thirty or so teenagers who already played in their high school bands. The band enjoyed considerable local success and spawned the even more popular Hurricane Brass Band, carried on into the late seventies as the Younger Fairview Band and then, for political reasons, as the Charles Barbarin Sr. Memorial Band. In 1983, Danny Barker did it again with the Roots of Jazz Brass Band, a venture that grew out of the Tambourine and Fan youth center on Hunter's Field. During that time, the number of musicians who passed through these bands was quite astonishing. There was Leroy Jones, Gregg Stafford, Anthony Lacen, Joe Torregano, Revert Andrews, Lucien and Charles Barbarin, Daryl Adams, Gregory Davis, Wynton and Branford Marsalis, Michael White, Eddie Bo Parish, Nicholas Payton, Efrem Towns, Gerry Anderson, William Smith, Kirk and Charles Joseph, Kevin Harris, James Andrews, and many more. Small wonder that Joe Torregano said of Danny Barker, "That group saved jazz for a generation in New Orleans," and Walter Payton added, "Danny Barker was like the Christopher Columbus of brass band music. He planted some good seeds." Veteran bandleader Harold Dejan was even more fulsome: "Now, Danny Barker needs some credit for the Fairview Band. He started that little band with the children. All the boys that played with him; the fellows of the Fairview Band should honor Danny Barker. They should give him a plaque or a trophy or something, because all those boys he really stuck with."[14]

Danny Barker's name crops up in many of the interviews in this book as someone who would encourage anyone who, in his estimation, was helping the cause of New Orleans music. It's this kind of activity rather than his earlier distinguished career as a musician that ensured his iconic status in the city today.

Unlike many of the musicians of his generation, he was staunchly supportive of the newer sounds created by the younger brass bands. Emile Martyn remembers just how supportive He explained to me:

Fairview Baptist
Church
Photo by Barry Martyn

I remember being with Danny Barker in Jackson Square, walking towards the river. I'd been playing in the afternoon with Tuba Fats. There was an English trombone player with us, and he was running down what he called the "modern music" played by "kids"; this would have been in 1985.

Danny sort of jumped on him; he wouldn't suffer fools gladly! He took off his hat and laid down his jacket and briefcase, as though he was stripping down for a fight. He said that he himself had a lot to do with the young bands—he didn't ever use the word "kids." He mentioned that he'd had a place where they all came and played, and he'd started them off on the road.

Danny said, "You don't realize, you guys that come here. The music changes, and these youngsters want to play something that belongs to today. They're playing the traditional tunes, but they're tightening them up.

"Everything's getting condensed. The drums are getting a tighter sound—they're tuning the snares tighter—it's more staccato. Modern influences and recording techniques mean they're after a cleaner sound, with a distinct beginning and end." He talked about the way the young bands dressed, T-shirts and baseball caps. They didn't want to be up there in black and white because for them, that was the past.

Danny was extremely aware of all that, and he was very defensive of young bands.

In 1973, Al Torregano, proprietor of the Jive Record Shop on North Claiborne, published *Jive,* a weekly newsletter. The issue of June 22 carried the following article on the Fairview band.

WHAT IS THE PARADE FOR?

Booooom, booooom.

Here comes the parade.

"What's the parade for?"

"What does it matter? Let's get in the second line and have some fun."

And so it goes. In New Orleans everybody loves a parade. We parade for Santa Claus, St. Patrick, Carnival, the Heart Fund, the Cancer Society, Spring Fiesta, funerals, and just about any other excuse we can think of. And no parade would be complete without one or two jazz marching bands.

Onward. Olympia. Eureka. Tuxedo. Immortal names in New Orleans. Marching bands unique to the Crescent City. Each band has been heaped with honors from coast to coast as well as at home. Each band is famous in its own right.

But have you heard about the Fairview Baptist Church Christian Band? No. Well, it's time you were told.

"The Fairview Baptist Church Christian Band is a marching band made up of 26 youngsters between the ages of nine and eighteen," explains Danny Barker, the band's organizer and a fine jazz musician in his own right. "We play all of the old jazz classics; we march in parades; we are good, and I don't mind bragging a little bit."

Started more than a year ago, the band is now in such demand that it rarely misses a street parade. "My people have always loved music," says Barker. "Most of us are born with the 'Baptist beat'—the rhythm of the good old Christian songs like *A Closer Walk with Thee*. We don't have to be taught a bunch of fancy stuff to be able to play an instrument. We go around with the melodies in our heads from the time we are just little folks and by the time we get our hands on an instrument and somebody shows us a thing or two, we are ready to play."

Leroy Jones Jr., a bright 14-year-old lad, did just that. His parents gave him a trumpet and before long he was blowing away like a junior Gabriel. He invited some of his friends over with their instruments and the Jones' garage on St. Denis Street was turned into a rehearsal hall.

"I used to walk down the street and listen to Leroy and his friends playing rock music," Barker explains, "and I got to thinking that they should be playing jazz." Barker spoke to Reverend Andrew Darby Jr., pastor of his church, Fairview Baptist, and they came up with the idea of trying to get the young people of the community interested in a Christian band. "Reverend Darby was very concerned about getting the youth in our community involved in worthwhile projects," Barker says.

Leroy liked the idea of forming a marching band. He talked to his friends and before long Barker had a dozen recruits. "We thought it was pretty great that he had Baptists, Catholics, Lutherans, Seven Day Adventists, and Holy Rollers playing in the Fairview Baptist Church Christian Band," he proudly states. "Gospel jazz music brought all of these young boys together with a single purpose: playing an instrument for a pastime rather than getting involved in some of the street problems of their peers."

Barker enlisted the help of Charlie Barbarin Sr., brother of the famous jazz trumpet player, Paul [actually a drummer], who passed away a few years ago. Barbarin, an able trumpet player himself, brought along his two young sons and became director of the band.

Leroy's parents agreed to allow the band to use their garage for practice; Reverend Darby cooperated by providing the church bus for transportation; Barbarin turned out to be a dynamic director; Barker took care of all the details; the boys supplied the music. The band began practicing each Monday night for three hours and soon invitations for personal appearances began to pour in.

"We just believed in the youngsters," says Barker. "We considered the band a self-help program where young boys could learn to do something for themselves; they could learn to follow directions; they could work towards a positive goal."

The group has played for both the 1971 and 1972 Jazz and Heritage Festival, and the Rag Time Jazz Festival in Washington, D.C. "We were also invited to play at the Celebration of Life, the Rock Festival in Pointe Coupee Parish," says Barker. "However, that was quite a mistake. When the band got there and saw all of the naked and half-naked people roaming around, their eyes nearly popped out of their heads and they scattered and ran down to the river to get a better look. We had a time getting them back together and out of the place."

One of the recent engagements the band especially enjoyed was playing for Mrs. Lucille Armstrong, the wife of the famous trumpeter Louis Armstrong, during her recent visit to Milne Boys Home. Mrs. Armstrong was in town to dedicate a portrait of her famous husband; the Fairview Band was on hand to provide the music for the occasion.

It was the second visit to the Home for the young band. When the group first started they went over to play at Milne, and the boys at the Home decided that they would also love to have a band. Now Milne also has a promising young jazz band.

The fame of the young Fairview band is spreading fast. Floyd Levin, a founder member of California Jazz Club, heard the band during the Jazz Festival and he persuaded his fellow club members to donate enough money to buy more than a dozen instruments for the group and to purchase caps and name bands. Durel Black, founder of the Louisiana Jazz Club and Music Therapy Fund, has also been a big supporter of the band; he has donated money for instruments.

"Of course, we still need more instruments," Barker explains. "We have so many young boys that would love to play in the band, but they are from poor families and they just can't afford an instrument."

Isn't he afraid that he may end up with too many musicians?

"No, that will never happen. If we get too big for one marching band we will form the second and then the third band. I can't think of a better way to help a youngster get off to the right start; music can make a difference.

"We need any new or old instruments we can get. Just call Reverend Darby at 949-4902 if you have an instrument around the house going to waste. I promise you that it will be put to good use."

Now when we speak of the famous marching bands, the list will have to read like this: Onward, Olympia, Eureka, Tuxedo, and the Fairview Baptist Church Christian Band.

Leroy Jones, Trumpet

BORN: New Orleans, February 20, 1958

Founding member of the Fairview band; leader of the Hurricane Brass Band and currently of his own quintet

Interviewed at the Palm Court Café, Decatur Street, September 2001

Courtesy Leroy Jones

I started playing music at the age of ten in the school band at St. Leo the Great School. I took the cornet, and the flute as my second choice, in case I didn't like the cornet.

My first teacher was Sister Mary Hillary, who was a trumpet player and a bandmaster at the school, a parochial school here in New Orleans. I started in the band in the fifth grade. I learned music from a conservatory method. I had lessons. I learned to read at the same time as I learned to play the horn. My parents had rented a used one because there was no point in buying a brand new one; if I hadn't been interested, they'd have wasted their money. Anyway, within three months, I had developed an embouchure, and my teacher had noticed I had a very good ear and a higher musical aptitude than a lot of the other kids who were my contemporaries. So my teacher suggested that my parents should buy me a new horn at the end of the year. The teacher noticed that when I was warming up, and when I was in the fifth grade, I was reading music at an eighth-grade level, so she knew I had some musical talent. My parents weren't musicians, so they couldn't determine that for themselves. The only other musician in my family was a cousin of mine who played trombone, not professionally but in the Fairview band, but we'll get to that later.

I also had a girl cousin who played the clarinet all through college; she was more classically trained. To this day, she can't play by ear to save her soul, and she can't understand how I do it. I don't understand it either. It's not something you think about, you know? But fortunately, I read as well, so I'm not limited to just one situation.

At twelve years old, my family moved from our old address on Buchanan Street to 1316 St. Denis Street. It was approximately sixty yards from the Fairview Baptist Church. I was raised Catholic, but I was influenced heavily by the Baptist tradition and hearing gospel and so forth because of the music at Fairview Church. Eventually, I met

21

Danny Barker, who lived just around the corner from my house. Also, Ernie Cagnolatti, and Dave "Fat Man" Williams lived just nearby. I grew up with Cag's grandkids. And the neighborhood was full of youngsters that played in school bands, unlike today, when the music programs are a bit slack.

It was much better in the late sixties and into the seventies. It's like, the bands that played Dixieland and the traditional jazz on Bourbon Street sort of diminished going into the eighties, long before I ever went there. I've spoken to some of the older musicians, and they told me how vibrant the street was with bands in those days. I even caught the tail end of that, playing at a club that had three bands a night—in fact, most of the clubs had three bands a night. Anyway, I first met Danny Barker in 1971.

I used to practice in my garage for five hours in the evening when I came home from school. At ten, I had to close it. So I'd do my homework and start practicing about five. I'd maybe take a break when my mom would call me in around seven. Otherwise, I'd play until ten. My dog used to howl in the alley when I played my horn—I don't know if it's because I sounded good or if I annoyed the hell out of him.

It didn't seem hard work: I just loved it so much. I don't practice that hard today, because I've developed a technique that means I don't have to practice that much to keep my endurance up. But for the first five to ten years of my development, I never practiced less than four hours every day. I would practice out of the Arban method book. I had private lessons at the weekend with Sister Mary Hillary and with a local trumpet player called Dalton Rousseau, also Laurence Winchester, who was one of the instructors at St. Augustine High School, where I went to in 1972.

I got to meet some local trumpet players through knowing Danny Barker. Some of my favorites were Jack Willis and Teddy Riley and our neighbor Ernie Cagnolatti. And I always loved Louis Cottrell's clarinet playing. They were all early influences on me, as well as the recordings that I had, or that my parents had—they played a lot of music in the house; they loved it, even though they weren't musicians.

They had some Louis Armstrong records, so I heard Louis before I even picked up a musical instrument. I'd been fooling with guitar before I started playing a wind instrument—I played the guitar for maybe ten years, which overlapped with the time I was playing cornet. I'm pretty much a self-taught guitarist—I never worked as a guitar player. I'd practice fingering and chord charts; then I'd do things on the horn. So I developed an understanding of harmony. I studied harmony a bit more, much later.

That neighborhood I grew up in was just so rich with music, just in that one-block radius. I never heard Jack Willis before he had his stroke, but I can imagine how great he was when he had all his faculties, because he still sounded great when I heard him. He remembered me as a little fellow, because we did things with Danny and the Fairview band when we traveled out of town and we were the youngsters.

The Fairview band was the brainchild of Reverend Andrew Darby and Danny Barker. Reverend Darby wanted to start a youth group for the Fairview Church. Danny and Blue Lou were members of the church. Of course, the pastor and congregation knew that Danny was a musician and Lou was a singer. So the pastor asked if they could involve some young musicians. Danny used to drive around the neighborhood—I'd often see him. I'd have the garage door open when I would be practicing. Or I'd have some friends with me that played in the school band.

There was a young man called Ronald Evans who played baritone. He's the nephew of Chuck Carbo, the singer. They lived nearby. Ronald used to practice with me and a drummer by the name of Raymond Johnson—we called him "Puppy." We used to get in there and jam. My parent's old stereo was in the garage, and we had LPs and 45s—even the odd 78. I used to buy them on the corner from Miss Wheeler, who was a friend of the family. We'd play along with the records. When I'd come back from my lesson, I'd go through the book—lesson 1, lesson 2—which I hated. I much more enjoyed sitting trying to emulate Louis Armstrong or Freddie Hubbard or Jack Willis or Shorty Rodgers—any instrumentalist. It didn't have to be trumpet players; I was trying to play everything I heard.

Anyway, Danny got out of his car one day and came up and introduced himself. I was pleased to meet him and quite flattered as well. He told me they had a plan to start a brass band. It was referred to as a youth group, and it was something to keep the neighborhood kids off the street. Because some of my peers were, I'd have to say, "bad boys"—through no fault of their own, they just weren't as fortunate as I was to have parents who really cared for them. So the Fairview band started, with mainly neighborhood kids. There were the Mimms brothers, Thomas and Gene. Thomas is a doctor now; I don't know what Gene's doing. I haven't seen those guys in years. They don't play music anymore.

Derek Cagnolatti, Ernie's grandson, was a member. He played alto saxophone. And there was Daryl Wilkinson on alto saxophone who lived next door. He was a little older than the rest of us, in his mid teens. And Raymond Johnson, "Puppy," was four years older than I. My cousin Isaac Banks, trombone player, we pulled him into the band. Harry Sterling—he's now the guitar player with Big Al Carson—back then, he played sousaphone as well as guitar and banjo. There was another trumpet player by the name of Morris Carmbs; he was a member of the church. There was also a young man by the name of Gary Proctor. He played trumpet. There was a kid called Nasser Adams. A tuba player called Stephen Parker was there in the beginning. Also Gregg Stafford, who came in on trumpet not long after, maybe a month after the band was formed. Mr. Barker had been working with Gregg. He's a little older than I am, so he was already on the scene in the French Quarter and so forth. When Danny pulled Gregg, Gregg pulled Tuba Fats. Joe Torregano joined us, and Herlin Riley played trumpet in those days. His mom used to drop him off at my house for rehearsals.

We had a guy called Ray Paisant—he's a Creole guy—he was kin to the Barbarins. That's how I met Lucien and Charles Barbarin. When Mr. Barker brought them into the band, Lucien was playing snare drum in those days. Greg Davis came in later, just before the band broke up.

At one point the Fairview band was almost thirty members. We had enough musicians to do three gigs on the same day in different places, and sometimes that's just what we did. Big Al Carson came into the band, as well as Stephen Parker and Tuba Fats, so we had three tuba players. We had maybe six trumpets. We had clarinets. There was a guy called "Dusty." I can't remember his right name—he was at school with Lucien—he played E-flat clarinet. Daryl Adams played alto sax. So we'd split the band up, because it was just too much sound. Work mainly came through word of mouth. Gregg Stafford would pull people in, like Michael Myers on trombone. He's dead now; he committed suicide in the eighties. He was from uptown, like Gregg. The rest of us were from downtown.

We were rolling—I mean, we had a trip up to Washington, D.C., round about 1972. We went up there with Fats Houston and the Olympia. The Onward Brass Band went. We all went up to play at the Kennedy Center for some function that was in honor of New Orleans music. My mother and Charles Barbarin Sr. would chaperone us, and of course Danny would come to keep us in line—we were all juveniles. It wasn't any problem: we were always basically just interested in playing.

We had a chance to appear in a movie with Tim Rooney, who's Mickey Rooney's son; he's kind of an amateur trombone player. They filmed that in the Quarter, all due to Danny's connections. He bent over backwards for us, and he really had a great affection for kids. He and his wife loved children.

The band was like a pet project for him, and that's why I couldn't understand when people started accusing him of exploiting us. The union accused him, and that was how the Hurricane Brass Band came about in 1974. By then I was sixteen; Danny had taught me how to deal with business, like "Make sure you get your contract straight, always count your money, make sure you get a deposit."

We played every weekend. We were the hottest thing on the second line circuit. All of the social and pleasure clubs wanted the Fairview band and then, later, the Hurricane Brass Band. We created such a stir that the Olympia Brass Band, in particular, were getting jealous of us. Danny had to stop being associated with us because of the flak from

Hurricane Brass Band at George "Kid Sheik" Cola's birthday party, September 1973 (Anthony Lacen, Kid Sheik, Daryl Adams, Leroy Jones, Greg Stafford) *Photo by Bill Dickens*

the union. A false rumor was generated by some musicians who were jealous of what was going on, and it made the scene difficult for Danny. We weren't all in the union, but some of the older guys were. At that time the AFM [American Federation of Musicians] was very strict about nonunion labor, or "scabs," as they called us.

Danny gave us the name [for the Hurricane Brass Band]. He said, "Y'all come down the street blowing like a hurricane." That's what gave us the name. I was the leader of the Fairview. Danny saw leadership qualities in me when I was thirteen years old. He saw I was a serious young man, and very focused, which is probably how I could practice four or five hours a day. So when the Hurricane band formed, I did the business for that, in conjunction with Gregg Stafford, who would cover for me if I wasn't available.

Gregg and I were very tight with that. We were the commanders of that group. We're very different musically, but at that time we were playing brass band music. We had people like Henry Freeman, a saxophone player who had been on the road with Ray Charles. He was a professional, man. He had been up to Baton Rouge, played in that [Southern University] Jaguar band; he knew Alvin Batiste—I mean, he could play, you know. So he was like a big influence. Magic Johnson, he came with the Hurricane. We had people like that coming in. I learned a lot from them. I mean, they knew music, not only just playing, but from a theoretical standpoint as well. I kept my mouth shut and my ears open, because I was absorbing a lot of information from these people.

Then Greg Davis and the Joseph brothers, Kirk and Charles, joined the Hurricane. Then Kevin Harris came along. So part of the core of the Dirty Dozen Brass Band were in the Hurricane at one time. We started to play original stuff, juxtaposing the funk and pop music with the traditional stuff. Later on, the Dirty Dozen took it to the next level.

In 1976, I branched off from the brass band thing and started playing rhythm and blues. The Hurricane still did gigs up to 1980, but then I got so involved with Bourbon Street, and I had a music scholarship to Loyola. I went there for a semester and dropped out because I didn't like the program and wanted to make some money. My parents were going through changes. They eventually busted up when I was nineteen, so I wanted to get out of the house. So I got my first jazz gig in the Quarter at the age of twenty at the Maison Bourbon in 1978. It was Dixieland and swing.

The job I took over was Jabbo Smith's spot. The One Mo' Time show came out, and Jabbo went up to New York with the show. That opened up the gig. Walter Payton was on bass with us, Joe Lambert on drums. That's when I started singing. Nobody else in the band sang. I started learning two or three tunes a week, including singing and scatting. I used to scat a lot, from listening to Jabbo and Thomas Jefferson.

It was great fun. It was exciting. It was just nice to be playing music. At the end of the week, you would be paid cash money, didn't have to pay taxes or nothing. I moved into the Quarter and got an apartment. There was music everywhere, and all the clubs had jazz. I played the Famous Door with Olivia Charlot [Cook]. Me and Lucien Barbarin hooked up together again in 1980, working for June Gardner and other people.

Then I formed my own quintet. We played at the old Paddock Lounge, and a bunch of other clubs up and down the street, for a limited amount of time because they were firing bands left and right. There were so many bands they could choose from. The first quintet I had was me and Lucien, trumpet and trombone. Then I had a young man who had gone to high school with me, Kenneth Sara, on drums. On piano I had James Moore—he doesn't live here anymore, but he was from New Orleans. And on bass, I had Joe Payton. And after that, I had Herlin Riley on drums, before he went out with Ahmad Jamal. Then I had Erving Charles on Fender bass, and on piano I had Phil Parnell. Then I got Shannon Powell after Herlin left. Then Richard Knox on piano, then Walter Payton on bass.

We made our first trip to Europe in 1982. It was great. I had started playing with the Louisiana Repertory Jazz Ensemble in 1980. I played on that record they did, Alive and Well. *I went to La Rochelle in France with them in May 1982, and in November, I went to Holland with my own quintet. I was twenty-four years old. I was so excited I didn't even feel jet lag.*

We got appreciation like I'd never seen before. I'd never seen people react to jazz music the way they did there. Bourbon Street was nice, and you'd get these people, and they'd get drunk and all of that, but this was sincere. That struck me. I felt like "I want to come back here again and again." And of course, I have been.

Back in the States, I carried on working the clubs in New Orleans. Then in 1983 I went up to Vancouver and spent three months working with Eddie "Cleanhead" Vinson. He was playing alto saxophone and singing, and I was with him at Gastown in Vancouver. I was up there with Shannon Powell—he had a lot of contacts up there, so we started working with different bands.

I came back in 1983, and they were getting ready to hold the World's Fair the following year, in 1984. The people that were behind the scenes for the organization were getting together a band called the Musical Ambassadors—this band was to go around promoting the Festival—they called it "A Year to Go." Charlie Bering was the guy that had that club, Lu and Charlie's. He was a great jazz lover and promoter of New Orleans music. Charlie got the band together, which consisted of myself, Phil Parnell, Walter Payton; Banu Gibson and Jeannie Ann Howell were the singers. On trombone was a guy called "Professor Gizmo"—I can't think of his right name. We were a show band, played a bit of everything. We all sang, all had choreography and everything. Most of the charts were heads, and we played a few stocks.

Then in '84 the fair opened up and we played there a little bit. Then the Intercontinental Hotel opened, and at that time I was married to a young lady from Australia that I had met at Maison Bourbon back in '78. She had a connection with the general manager of the Intercontinental, so I got to open at Pete's Pub, with a quartet. I also got to play with Della Reese for the grand opening. I had Shannon Powell on drums, Rusty Gilder on bass, and Ed Frank on piano. We were there for a year. It was a good gig. I was also playing at the newly opened Mahogany Hall, which used to be the Paddock Lounge. This was with me and Shannon, David Grillier on clarinet, Maynard Chatters on trombone; Mary Mayo was the singer, Emile Vinet on piano, and Curtis Mitchell on bass. My marriage was breaking up, but things were looking good from a business point of view. The Pete's Pub gig folded, and the hotel started a jazz brunch on Sundays.

In 1985, I left to go to Singapore with Trevor Richards and the Camelia Jazz Band. Trevor was on drums, Pud Brown on reeds, Quentin Batiste on piano. They opened in this five-star hotel. So I turned the brunch gig over to Lucien Barbarin, since I was going to be gone for three months. It ended up being over a year, because the gig was so successful that they renewed the contract. The first six months we had a chef from New Orleans. It was called the New Orleans Restaurant, very exclusive. Six nights a week, tuxedos every night.

In January 1986, Pud went home because his wife wasn't too well. Quentin Batiste went home too—he was homesick. So Ed Frank came in on piano and Charlie Gabriel on clarinet.

We went on to play in Jakarta, Indonesia. I came home in September '86, stayed for two weeks, and went again for nine months. Kuala Lumpur for a month, three weeks in the Philippines, and on to Manila. Then Bangkok, Taiwan, Hong Kong. Whenever we went to Indonesia, we'd stay three months in Jakarta. This went on all the way up until 1989. So I was in Asia for about four years.

Then I hooked up with L. D. Young and Red Hope; that was the original Ramsay Lewis Trio. I met the guitarist Ernie Raglin, who was associated with the Jamaican pianist Monty Alexander. We did some recording together. We did a record called the Jazz Ambassadors with Lillian Boutté.

When I came back, I'd really matured musically. We did this recording, and I'll never forget Lucien Barbarin saying, "Wow, Leroy's made it." I did some gigs at Maison Bourbon, and I worked around with Wanda Rouzan. We played at the Meridien Hotel in Paris.

Then I got a call from Harry Connick Jr.'s management. In May 1990, I went to play on the Brussels Jazz Rally, for a very nice guy called Jacques Cruyt—unfortunately now deceased. I got back from Belgium in early June and started rehearsing up in Princeton with the Harry Connick Orchestra. Harry had hit big with the motion picture soundtrack for When Harry Met Sally.

That band gave me really great exposure that I hadn't had before here in the United States. I fulfilled the same kind of role as Harry ["Sweets"] Edison in the Nelson Riddle Orchestra. We had a chart for "More" where I played what Sweets had played behind Frank Sinatra. It was the exact same Quincy Jones chart.

At that time, I was in my second marriage. I had married a local young lady this time. Six months after I got married, I was on the road, so you can imagine what happened to that marriage! The big band headed to the top; then Harry switched to doing more commercial music. He did a record called She, and I performed on that as well.

I got my first record deal on a major label because of Harry Connick Jr. He formed a record company that got distribution from Columbia. It was called More Cream from the Crop, and it was released in 1995. The next year I did Props for Pops, which was a tribute to Louis Armstrong, released in 1996. If it were not for Harry, I would not have had that opportunity. He had a lot of faith and confidence in me, and great respect for me as a musician.

Since 1996, I've recorded several times with him and with other artists. I haven't had the opportunity to record as leader, but that's in the makings. Now, in 2001, I still work with Harry, and I've done some recording with some European friends of mine, including the Danish Radio Big Band. I'm still totally in love with music. It's a blessing to play for audiences and for them to appreciate it.

Anthony "Tuba Fats" Lacen, Bass Horn

BORN: New Orleans, September 15, 1949

Played with Doc Paulin, Nat Dowe, the Hurricane Brass Band, the E. Gibson Brass Band,
and Dejan's Olympia Brass Band; founder and leader of the Chosen Few Brass Band

Interviewed at his home on Dumaine Street, October 2002

Photo by Marcel Joly

The neighborhood I came up in was a family neighborhood, on Simon Bolivar. Everybody on the block stayed at my momma's house. All the kids were raised right there. We all played together on the porch. It was just a big family house.

My father used to hunt. We had hunting dogs and chickens and goats. Everybody on that block was from either Mississippi or Alabama. They had come to New Orleans to work the riverfronts, which was a blooming thing then. My mother would cook big pots of stuff; everybody ate greens and cornbread, fatback, ham hocks, all that stuff. My mother was from Georgia. She picked in the fields when she was a kid, so it was country cooking.

Soul food. Everybody in the street would bring a plate, and she would feed everybody.

When I was a kid, before integration, there was this place called the White Castle, had these little small hamburgers with onions and cheese on them. They were only a nickel apiece. We couldn't go to the front of the White Castle because we were black—we had to go to the back window. My sisters would give me their nickels, and I'd go to the back and get them. We'd go in the backyard and eat them. My mother caught us with a whole box. She took them from us and threw them in the garbage can and threw some to the dogs. She said, "I don't care how mad you get. You shouldn't have gone there and bought them, because you can't go and sit in there and eat them. Go and buy your hamburgers from the black people." I said, "We don't want to. We want the White Castle burgers." My mother slapped me. She told me, as long as I live, don't answer her back, and don't ever go there and buy another hamburger. She was trying to make a point. It took me a long time to realize what she meant.

There were no fences between the houses, we all just shared. In later years, the fences came. As the older people died off and other people bought the properties, that's when the fences came. If somebody went out to the country, they'd come back with a hog and slaughter it. They'd cook it up in the yard and share it with everybody in the neighborhood. They'd have suppers in the backyard with a jukebox playing—yard parties.

My father would hunt in the parishes, but you didn't have to go that far. You could just go to New Orleans East and hunt—all that was woods and swampland back then. Now they built Jazzland, housing developments, shopping centers—you can't hunt down there no more. He would go to St. Bernard Parish, Jefferson Parish over the river. There were a lot of places to hunt.

My daddy must have had about fifty dogs at one time. They had pens in the yard for them. He had beagles, rabbit dogs, black and tick, bluetick hounds, all kinds of hunting dogs. My daddy worked on the riverfront. He'd bring home grits, mix up with some mash, feed the dogs. You could go to the Chinese restaurant—they didn't use the livers and the gizzards; they put out big boxes of that stuff. What we didn't use for the house, we'd put in a big pot in the yard, boil it up for the dogs. And go round the restaurants hustling scrap food. You fed dogs like you fed hogs—on anything.

I was running wild, falling off the houses and stuff. I used to throw the Times-Picayune *paper. There was a mortuary I had to deliver to. I used to throw the paper from my bike, but they told me I had to put the mortuary paper at the door—somebody had been taking their paper or something. I got off the bike and walked up to the door. I was just putting the paper down, when there was this knocking from the inside of the door.* BOOM! BOOM! BOOM! *I ran like hell and pissed all over myself!*

And there was an embalming studio right across from my house, on Simon Bolivar and Jackson, an old wooden building. Reb, the mortician, used to embalm the bodies in the back room there. We used to go get on the back fence and watch him working with the bodies in the back. He'd sneak round the side and catch us. "Get outta here, boy!" We'd run down the alley.

We used to call Dryades Street the black people's Canal Street. If you came to Canal Street in those days, you got a treat. This was segregation days. We shopped on Dryades, where the Jewish people had the stores. We didn't go to Canal Street because we didn't have the Canal Street prices. It was much cheaper uptown, like at the Big D department store. All that's gone now; the buildings are still there. They've made apartment houses out of them, and there's a black museum and stuff.

The river trade went down, the oil fields went down, the city went down. Now, they're trying to build the city on tourist business. All the trade started going down in the early seventies. Everyone worked as longshoremen—the biggest industry down here was the riverfront. All the steel companies were open. Up by the convention center, you can still see some of the stacks where the steel mills were.

There was live music all over the city. Down in the Tremé, there was the old Caldonia, Mama Ruth's Cozy Corner. The old Caldonia's gone, but they named another place the Caldonia. That's after Armstrong Park came through and they lost all that development in there. Joe's Cozy Corner used to be Mama Ruth's; Kid Sheik and them used to play in there. I used to go down on my bike and watch the funerals and things. The bands would start by Ruth's Cozy Corner. Actually, Harold Dejan was the first band that went in the Tremé to play jazz funerals. None of the other brass bands wanted to play funerals in the Tremé—they were frightened of it. The Tremé was always known for drugs and crime.

The ward I stayed in was the Third Ward, but they called it Central City—it's the center of the city of New Orleans. Where I lived was only about seven blocks from the Garden District. When I was a kid, I used to ride my bike and play up there—it was the hustling area. You needed money to go to a show, you go by the old folks' home on St. Charles, help the people with their groceries from the car to their apartment, they would give you a quarter or something like that. I played ball on the street, helped people rake their yards, cut grass. I had a push mower—it used to put blisters on the side of your hand; you had to put a glove on. If you were hustling, you wanted that money. I hustled soft drink bottles; the glass bottles were worth three cents.

I was always a kid that strayed away from home—I still do it. I was the black sheep, you know, I never stuck around the house. I would be told, "Don't leave," and the minute they turned their back, I was gone—especially if there was a funeral coming down the street.

There were musicians uptown and down. They had an organization called the Young Men's Olympia. They still do the jazz funerals uptown. There isn't that many musicians uptown anymore, but more of them are in the Tremé. The Tremé came back to reviving the music. When I was a kid, second lines were popular but not as popular as they are now. In those days, there were very few clubs parading, and the parade season would be September to November, and that would be it, unless you caught a jazz funeral or church parade for an anniversary.

There was organizations like the Oddfellows, Knights of Columbus, the Masons. They would have bands playing marches like "Gettysburg," "Bugle Boy," regular marches. They would be lined up in their uniforms with their swords, and they would drill. Face each other, side by side, walk into a semicircle, come back around, stuff like that. That was a treat to see, you got a chance to second line again. After a while, they'd turn the band loose and let them play "Whooping Blues."

When I was at junior high school, I had just started playing brass band music on the street, with the Gibson Brass Band, Doc Paulin, and a guy named Nat Dowe. The school band director and I got into an argument. I was about fourteen. He got on me because he wanted me to play the regular marches the school band was playing, and I would get carried away and play something swinging. He didn't like it. He got mad and told me, "I'm going to put you out of the band."

So they sent me to art class—I had no skills for that, none whatsoever. The teacher would put something on the desk for you to draw, give you sheets to draw on. I would sit there and write music on them! Her name was Miss Daniel; she was a very nice person. She told me, "Try to draw something." And I would draw a mountain—and I would make a bird like an "m." She told me, "No good, you're not going to make it in this class." So they took me back in the band. It was kicks.

I grew up watching musicians, and that's what I wanted to be. I even tried to play football. But I got hit one time too many, and I thought, "To hell with this. I'm going back to the band room."

The first bands I heard were Papa Celestin and Doc Paulin. I got to see all the blues cats like B. B. King, Bobby Blue Bland. Where I was born and raised was only six blocks from the Dew Drop. I would sneak out at night when my family would go to sleep; everybody would be tired from having to work hard all day, so it was easy. I wouldn't stay out all night, just a couple of hours. I would ease the bike out of the side door. See, I was big, I had hair on my chin, I looked older. Sometimes my mother would bust me!

In the neighborhood, we had the Dew Drop, the Robin Hood; Big Joe Turner's bar was on Jackson and Daneel. It's a rough place now—still a bar, called Tammy's Place. On a Sunday afternoon, me and my friends would go sit on the corner and listen to Big Joe Turner. He had piano, drums, bass, guitar, saxophone—a regular band. That's how I learned about the blues. Sometimes we'd go round there, and I'd ask his girlfriend, "Where Mr. Joe at?" She'd tell me they'd gone out of town for a couple of days. A week later, he'd be back sitting on that stool, singing. Man, he was good!

I know how to play rhythm and blues changes, as well as traditional changes. I had quite a few people taught me things. I used to listen at string bass players—that was my thing. When I started, I wanted to play trumpet. I used to cut a hose pipe up, put a funnel on the end, twist a mouthpiece in. Sounded just like a trumpet. Sam Alcorn, Old Man [Alvin] Alcorn, all them cats was playing around then, uptown. And Big Dowe was a

Dew Drop Café, 2840 La Salle Street. *Photo by Ralston Crawford. Courtesy Hogan Jazz Archive, Tulane University.*

hell of a trumpet player—if he had a brass band job, he would let visiting European musicians play with him. Him and my mother was good friends. One evening he saw me coming home from school with the tuba, playing it—they'd told me to take it home and practice. He said, "Come here, Anthony, sit here on the porch." He went and got his horn and started teaching me different scales and things. One Saturday, he said he had a gig for me, paid a dollar. I said, "I can't play this stuff." He said, "Just play what I tell you to play." He showed me what a shuffle rhythm was.

They would play for the Elks Club over by the river. These organizations would have suppers on Saturdays, and at night they would have a dance. He would have the band playing the dance, and his bass player would get drunk, so he would come and get me to play tuba. They played a lot of shuffle—he had good musicians with him—he even had Buddy Charles playing guitar with him; he showed me changes and stuff. He had Flo Anckle, David Grillier—they used to play up some music!

I did a whole lot of listening to Chester Zardis and Placide Adams at the Heritage Hall. I used to ride my bike down to Bourbon Street in the evenings, and I heard these cats, slapping these basses. That's where I got those turnarounds from.

For some reason, I started to play left handed—I even put the valves in reverse order. I didn't get the credit for bringing the swing to it—Kirk Joseph gets the credit for it. It came from me; I wanted to swing the band like an upright bass player.

By the time I got in with Danny Barker and the Fairview band, I was a grown man in my middle twenties—I'm fifty-two now. What happened, Gregg Stafford came to me. Danny needed somebody to play tuba with the band; the kids couldn't get the tuba together. So I shaved my beard off and went down there. After a year or so, Danny said, "Y'all getting too big now. You, Gregg, Leroy, some of you others, y'all get together and form the Hurricane Brass Band."

We were powerful, and that was when the swing started to hit the traditional music— I was the oldest one in the band. We started to get a lot of second lines and a lot of convention work, the Fairmont and stuff too. That's when I think Louis Cottrell, Harold Dejan, and Herman Sherman got together to split the band up. It got to the point where Gregg and Leroy were both playing with the Tuxedo; Joe Torregano and I went to the Olympia.

The music started changing in the seventies—Daryl Adams and those kids, they were thinking of different modern riffs. In 1974, that's when Milton started wanting to do different things with the Olympia, and Harold kept telling him, "No, we're not going to do that." That's when "Mardi Gras in New Orleans" happened. I'll never forget it: we were leading a Bacchus Parade on St. Charles. Then we got "I Got a Woman" together. That's when the Olympia started changing. We played my tune "Tuba Fats." How that came about, we were doing a parade, and when the band stopped, the second liners, with the tambourines and stuff, started singing "Hey Pocky Way"—the Indian song that the [Funky] Meters had recorded. So I started putting a bass part to it, and it became a song.

That's when I formed the Chosen Few Brass Band. Milton worked a bunch of second lines with us—I used to hire him and Edmund Foucher. We had Kermit [Ruffins] too, but he had to play with the Rebirth—they were just forming. So I would lose him. And I would hire Stackman or Freddie Kemp. We were really playing rhythm and blues with a brass band. It gave Milton a chance to play what he wanted, and we were already headed in that direction anyway. We would play the same tune for eight or twelve blocks.

The Rebirth wasn't as popular then; they got popular in the later years. I decided to get away from that. It was important to keep the traditional music going too—the guys in the Olympia were getting old, and there was room for another traditional brass band. There was a lot of work at conventions and stuff. Plus I was getting older, too.

But what really changed things was the Dirty Dozen. That band was a funny thing, really, it started as a joke. Once Sunday parades were over with, I went by the Caldonia bar to see what was going on. Benny Jones and them were all there; they were second lining to the jukebox, beating on the tables, dancing out the door—it was eleven o'clock in the morning!

They were all, "Hey, Tuba, get your horn!" And there was this trumpet player called Cyrille Salvant, he was a hell of a player. He was as drunk as a skunk, playing with

Chosen Few Brass Band (Eddie Bo Parish, Anthony Lacen, Elliott Callier, Benny Jones, Kenneth Austin, George Johnson) *Photo by Marcel Joly*

them. So I went and got my horn—me and Cyrille started to play along with the jukebox. Then all these other guys went home and got drums and stuff—they all lived right there in the neighborhood. So then we took it to the street.

Cats put on union drawers; they had all kind of like sticks with feathers on them and stuff. Somebody said, "Mama Ruth got a party—it's in the project by Goo's house." So we second lined over to the Lafitte project, and I stayed out all day playing with them.

So every Sunday after that, if somebody had a dance or a party in the Tremé, they'd say "Hey, Tuba! Come on out, we're going to pass the hat." So we struck up at the Caldonia, and we paraded all the way round the Tremé to that dance. But I was busy with the Olympia; I really didn't have time to stick with it, so I got Kirk Joseph to come and play instead. Then we brought his brother Charles in, then Roger Lewis, then Gregory Davis.

What happened, Roger showed Benny and them how they could make a brass band together. Fats Domino's work had started slowing down, and Roger wasn't working that much. They went to a secret rehearsal: Roger, Benny, Jenell Marshall the snare drummer, Kirk, Charles. They went to Frog's house—I think he was showing them how they could write things out, and how funky they could get, because he was there with them also. Then came the St. Joseph's Day parade. I was playing with the Olympia, and I saw

Roger and Benny and them coming. They told Lionel Batiste and them, "Y'all keep that band with the kazoos and stuff over there," and they wouldn't play with Lionel.

The Olympia headed up the parade, and I could see Lionel and them behind us. And I could also see a big crowd way behind them. I couldn't see exactly who it was, but when we got to Hunter's Field (on Claiborne and St. Bernard where the Tambourine and Fan was), there was Benny, Roger, Gregory Davis, Efrem Towns, Kirk—man, they were wailing! And fast. It took off from there.

I remember when they put the Interstate 10 over Claiborne—it got rid of the dust. With those trees on the neutral ground, no grass could grow, because of the shade. It would be dusty, dusty, dusty! Cats would kick up the dust dancing—you'd be covered. Then it got muddy when the freeway came through, but they still brought the parades through there.

OBITUARY IN *New Orleans Music* MAGAZINE, BY MICK BURNS
Anthony Lacen: Goodbye Tuba Fats
Born 15 September 1949; died 11 January 2004

Anthony Lacen (a.k.a. "Tuba Fats") was the eldest of five children. His parents, Johnny and Leola Lacen, had moved to New Orleans from Georgia to find work, and the family lived on Simon Bolivar in the Third Ward, in the area known as Central City.

As a child, he delivered newspapers and hustled in the nearby Garden District, where he did domestic chores for a few cents. Once he started to play tuba in the high school band, he had another hustle. A trumpet-playing neighbor, "Big" Nat Dowe, gave him some informal tuition on the porch of his house, and soon Tuba was playing on the street with bands led by Doc Paulin, Nat Dowe, and with the Gibson band. Dowe also had a dance band, which did a lot of work at the Elks Club over the river. The band included David Grillier, Buddy Charles, Flo Anckle, and a bass player who used to get drunk and not show up. Despite initial reluctance, Tuba was persuaded to join and was soon supplying the shuffle rhythms the band needed. This was the beginnings of his style and his unique contribution to bass horn playing—he wanted to play double bass on the tuba. Soon he was making nocturnal bicycle trips down to the French Quarter, listening to such as Placide Adams, Chester Zardis, and James Prevost—there were plenty of role models.

He was doing nothing in particular when Gregg Stafford recruited him for the Fairview Baptist Church Band, and the offshoot, The Hurricane Band. Then followed several years with Dejan's Olympia Brass Band, with whom, in 1976, he recorded "Tuba Fats"—the nickname bestowed upon him by Danny Barker during the Fairview days. In 1983, after leaving the Olympia, he formed his own Chosen Few and took up permanent residence in Jackson Square—he had a passionate belief in the integrity of the street musician. It was during this period that he became a role model for the young musicians who flocked to join him in the square—Keith Anderson, Kermit Ruffins, Dwayne Burns, and countless others. For several years, Tuba's wife, "Lady" Linda Young, sang with the band until her tragic early death from cancer in 1997. I don't think Tuba ever recovered from the loss.

I got to know him pretty well over the course of several years, and he toured three times with my band in Europe during 1995 and '96. He was capable of amazing generosity. During parade jobs, he would stoop over mesmerized children to give them candy he'd crammed into his pockets earlier. Once during a catfish supper at his Dauphine Street home, he produced several cans of English beer for me (he wasn't drinking at the time). He'd brought them back in his suitcase—he knew I didn't like the local beer much. He had his little phobias, he was afraid of heights and the dark. I remember him staring into the blackness from a country hotel window, and musing, "Mmm. Ain't nobody gotta tell Fats to stay his black ass in the house."

During the last few years of his life, he'd been "adopted" by Walt and Ronda Rose, who provided him with a subsidized apartment in Dumaine Street and made sure he got healthy food and medication for his heart condition. Whenever I got to New Orleans, Fats was always the first person I'd call. In January this year, I was in New Orleans to make a radio documentary about Harold Dejan. On Monday, January 12, Barry Martyn and I were leaving Barry's house on Burgundy Street at 10:40 A.M. A musician neighbor of Barry's, called David, crossed the street and said, "Did you hear about Tuba? He died last night from a heart attack. . . ."

Gallier Hall, St. Charles Avenue, January 18, 12:20 P.M. This is a venue for the funerals of local celebrities, and Tuba was certainly that. The bleachers are up for Mardi Gras, and it's crowded with people waiting to second line. By one of the doorways, there's a throbbing percussion section of plainclothes Mardi Gras Indians—Tuba was a Wild Magnolia in his youth. Inside, the huge ballroom is divided into roughly three parts: one for a small section of the parade band (only about fifteen pieces), one for the seated congregation and family, and a third for the standees and the dancers. In the last year, Tuba had apparently formed an association with the Sudan Social Aid and Pleasure Club, and twenty or so of them had turned out for this occasion— bright orange shirts, tan pants, sashes, umbrellas, unlit cigars, all dancing their asses off for Tuba Fats. The band plays "Just a Little While to Stay Here," "Lily of the Valley," "I'll Fly Away"—the congregation sings and cries. It's unbelievably moving.

Then outside to second line in front of the horse-drawn hearse. It's a huge crowd and a big band. I recognize Lionel Batiste Sr., Jenell Marshal, Roger Lewis, Benny Jones, Keith Anderson, Eddie Bo Parish, Revert Andrews, James Andrews, Leroy Jones, Doc Watson, Robert Harris, and Kermit Ruffins. It's too far away to hear who's playing, but at the back I count the bells of fourteen sousaphones. It's not a recipe for musical coherence, but it's an impressive tribute.

We move off, along Carondelet, over Canal and onto Bourbon Street. This is the first time I've walked through the French Quarter with Tuba without having to stop every two minutes while he talked to people—the barkers, the street people, musicians, the lady from the A&P, just about everybody. Turn right down St. Ann and into Jackson Square. In front of St. Louis Cathedral, three priests wait to bless the body as it passes; I can imagine what Tuba would have said. Then right again down St. Peter to turn the body loose at Preservation Hall.

Goodbye Tuba Fats.

Gregg Stafford, Trumpet

BORN: New Orleans, July 6, 1953

Played with the E. Gibson Brass Band, the Fairview Baptist Church Brass Band,
the Hurricane Brass Band, and the Young Tuxedo Brass Band

Interviewed at his home on Second Street, October 2002

Photo by Peter Nissen

I've lived here in New Orleans all my life, and I don't think I could accept living any-
where else. I don't think I'd be a musician today if I hadn't been born here, because of
the way circumstances happened in my life. Actually, I became a musician not by choice
but by fate. I guess it was predestined.

While I was between junior and senior high school, I was about fifteen years old.
I had always lived uptown, mostly two blocks away from where we're sitting now. My
mother and father had separated, and for a brief period I lived downtown at my mother's
new house on Burgundy Street. At that time, you had to attend the school that was in the
district where you lived. I had already selected industrial arts as one of my electives—I
was always good at drafting, measuring, and woodworking.

I had to get a false address and a permit to attend school uptown. While I was wait-
ing for it to come through, I didn't attend school at all for about six weeks; my mother got
the impression that I was somehow trying to drop out of school. She got up one morning
and said, "Look, this is your last day. If you can't get your school sorted out today, you're
going to have to go to either Booker T. Washington or Joseph Clark."

I went up to see the principal, and he told me, "I notice that one of your electives is industrial arts. That class has stopped, so I can offer you three choices: vocal music, instrumental music, or home economics." At that time, home economics was considered to be a female course, and I never did like the idea of singing in a choir.

The band director happened to be in the office while the principal was telling me this. When I left the office, he approached me and said, "Open your mouth!" I thought something was wrong with my teeth, so I looked at him kind of strangely. He said, "Just open your mouth, and grit your teeth. I want you to select instrumental music as your choice." I said, "I don't think I can do that, because I don't have an instrument." He told me, "Don't worry about that. I'll let you use one of the school instruments."

Prior to that, when I was in junior high school, I had asked my mother to buy me an instrument, because most of the kids in the neighborhood played. But she wouldn't get one, because she assumed that I would lose interest, and she would have wasted the money.

Of course, I had heard bands playing on the street, but I hadn't been inspired by a passion for music—that developed when I started to play. There was music all over the neighborhood where I lived. There were a lot of local musicians who were very prominent on the rhythm and blues scene. Ernie K. Doe lived locally, and Raymond Lewis, the bassist. I was only a few blocks from the Dew Drop, and just about every corner had a barroom where music was played. When I was a kid, you saw music everywhere.

I went home that night, and the first thing my mother wanted to know was whether I had got into school. I told her I had. She asked me had I got all my classes, and I said, "All except one. I had to make a choice, and I'm thinking of taking instrumental music." She flew into a rage. "I am not signing no paper for no instrument. No! No way." She thought that even if the school loaned me a horn, she would still be responsible for paying for it.

I went to school the next day, and the band instructor was waiting for me, with my horn. He said, "Did you make your selection?" I said, "My mother won't sign the slip." He said, "Tell her not to worry. Even if you lose the horn, she doesn't have to pay for it."

I told my mother what he had said that night, but she still refused to sign. I cried all night—I didn't want to take vocal music, and I definitely didn't want to take home economics. My mother would get up at six o'clock in the morning to go to work. She had heard me crying in the night, and she came to my room. She said to me, very reluctantly, "I'm going to sign that slip for you. But you tell that band instructor that I'm not going to be responsible for any instrument."

I went to school with the consent slip, gave it to the band instructor—Solomon Smith was his name (we called him Fess). I was under the impression that you got to choose your instrument, and I wanted to play the tenor saxophone. But when we got to the band room, he said, "What you want doesn't come into it. You're playing trumpet because that's what I need, to play second and third parts." He went in the back of the band room

GREGG STAFFORD, TRUMPET 41

Johnny Wimberley
Courtesy Hogan Jazz Archive, Tulane University

and got me a beat-up, tarnished cornet. I liked the sound of it. It wasn't in bad shape; it was just old, and at the time, people were using trumpets. I think that cornet had been around since the school opened in the early fifties. That's how I got started. I think, because of my Christian faith, it was preordained. Some things are appointed.

Growing up in this part of New Orleans, I lived right around the corner from Shakespeare Park, where the church parades and the Elks parade started from. Just about every Sunday there'd be a parade. You'd see Doc Paulin, the Reliance Brass Band, and the E. Gibson Brass Band. Second lining was a fun thing to do after church.

By the time I had finished beginner's classes, the instructor was ready to put me in the school band, playing third parts. We were playing for Tulane homecoming—that was a big thing at that time. They would have the bands of several different schools, and there would be a display of formation marching at half time. After the parade, some of us were walking to the trolley stop. There were some members of the E. Gibson band getting into their cars. The leader of the band, Johnny Wimberley, stopped us and said, "You young fellows—any of y'all be interested in playing our kind of music?" My friends in the band were mostly reed players or trumpet players. The saxophone players weren't interested, but I enjoyed watching the brass band trumpet players. I'd seen Milton Batiste, and I'd seen the Onward band a few times. So I asked him if he needed trumpet players. He said they didn't, except sometimes they might need an extra trumpet. I gave him my name and telephone number.

I had a friend called Michael Myers, a trombone player. He was playing with bands, and Tuba Fats was playing with Doc Paulin and the E. Gibson band. I knew Tuba from the neighborhood, but I didn't know him personally. I had grown up with Michael Myers—we had even gone to the same nursery. He was playing with the E. Gibson band. I got a phone call one evening from Johnny Wimberley. He said they had an Elks parade coming up, and could I go to rehearsals on Thursday nights to learn some of the tunes. They were putting out two bands for the Elks parade—I would be in the same band as Mr. Wimberley.

By then, I would be sixteen years old. Marching in the parades with the high school band at that time, when you had on your uniform, that was something special. We'd compete for trophies in the Mardi Gras parades, so you were concentrating on staying in tune, trying to keep the line straight, all that. The other guys in the trumpet section of my high school band were all good sight-readers. And at that time, I had only one year left to do at high school. I really had no idea that music was to become my second source of livelihood.

I became a part of the E. Gibson band. When you follow parades, you hear Doc Paulin playing tunes like "Margie" and "By and By," "Closer Walk"—you get used to hearing those tunes, and I'd go home and learn them. There were two guys in the Gibson band; their mother was a very close friend of my grandmother. They grew up in the Magnolia housing project. So that, and my friendship with Michael Myers, meant that I felt very comfortable in that band. I learned the songs, and I started my brass band apprenticeship.

A year later, I met Danny Barker. I had finished high school in the summer of 1971, and I was working at a place called Purkiss Pancake Parlor, which was an all-night restaurant on Bourbon Street. All the musicians and police officers and strip girls would come in there when they finished work—Bourbon Street still had its charm then. I would see the captain of police first, then Thomas Jefferson would come in, and Louis Prima—I saw a lot of musicians who were working on the street. I worked in the kitchen; I was working my way through college. I got to know the night people—the policemen, the girls, the musicians, waiters, and barkers from the different clubs.

Dixieland Hall was right across the street. On my breaks, I'd go across and listen to Louis Cottrell, Jeanette Kimball, Jack Willis—those guys would be playing there. It was an extension of the brass band music I was playing uptown. I'd seen Jack Willis and Alvin Alcorn playing parades. "Showboy" Thomas would come in with Thomas Jefferson for breakfast. Tom was working everywhere—he was at the Paddock Lounge, Maison Bourbon, the Famous Door. He was working three jobs a day.

I had got to know Worthia "Showboy" Thomas a little bit, and he knew I was playing with the Gibson band uptown. He said, "Oh, you're working with those scab bands." He started working with George Finola at Maison Bourbon. By then, Danny Barker had started the Fairview Church band. I had seen them once, when they played at the Southern Christian Music Conference in New Orleans. They marched from St. Bernard and Claiborne all the way to Shakespeare Park.

This was around 1972—after Martin Luther King's assassination. Black people were looking for leadership. Jesse Jackson had started his PUSH organization, and everybody was going in different directions. The parade at the conference was like a "come together" parade—the idea was for everyone to gather in Shakespeare Park.

I met the parade as it was coming into Simon Bolivar, just where we call it the borderline between uptown and downtown. They had the Olympia Brass Band, the Young

Tuxedo, and the Fairview Baptist Church band. That was the first time I heard Leroy Jones—I had never heard a trumpet player with such a good sound. I only saw them that one time, but I was impressed.

Sometime later I was talking to Showboy at the restaurant, and he said, "I have this friend called Danny, who has this little church band. You might want to join them. Would you be interested in meeting them? I don't know the name of the band—they're a group of kids." Then I knew who he was talking about.

He brought Danny Barker down to meet me two nights later. I took their coffee to the table, and Showboy said, "This is Mr. Danny Barker. This is that friend I've been telling you about." Danny looked at me and said, "I understand you play an instrument. I have a group of young musicians—it's called the Fairview Baptist Church band. I'm trying to keep them off the streets, keep them out of trouble, trying to preserve the old music. Showboy tells me you play uptown, with the Gibson band. Do you know some of those old songs?" I said I knew "Just a Little While," "By and By," "The Saints," "Lord, Lord, Lord." He said, "OK, that's enough. You'd be a good help. Would you be interested in playing? Would it interfere with your job?" I explained that I was working my way through college. He said, "So you're an ambitious young man—that's good."

He told me that they rehearsed in Leroy Jones's garage on St. Denis Street every Thursday night. "It's down by the St. Bernard project." he said. "Do you know how to get down there? You got transportation? We've got a job coming up for a campaign, and we need to rehearse for it." I had a nice little car that I had saved up to buy, and Danny was quite impressed when I pulled up in it. He introduced me to the guys: there was Lucien and Charles Barbarin, Leroy, Derek Cagnolatti, about twelve of them in the garage.

Leroy and I hit it off real good. The way Mr. Barker would rehearse, there was never any music. He would bring records for us to listen to. At the time, he was trying to get the band to learn "Weary Blues"—he brought sheet music for that one. A few of us were able to read it—he'd play it, and we'd listen. He'd say, "Listen at the melody."

A few weeks later, we went and played that campaign job. We had a good time together, and he split the money with us—he always made sure that everybody got something. That's how I became a member of the Fairview band, and Leroy was looking for some help anyway. Charles and Lucien Barbarin were the naggers of the band; they would try to do anything to discourage you, but in a fun way. They were the hell-raisers. We all became good friends.

Eventually I took Joe Torregano down there with me. Both of us were attending Southern University, and I knew him from there. He was playing with the Olympia Brass Band at the time. He told Tuba Fats about it, and he came down too. He had the experience, he had played with those uptown bands, and he had a lot of power.

Hurricane Brass Band, 1980 (Gregg Stafford, Lucien Barbarin) *Photo by Mike Casimir*

The band had a lot of strength, and I guess that's when certain people went to the musician's union about us, but I don't want to get into that. That's why Danny had to cut us loose, and that's how the Hurricane band came about. Danny came in, and he had had some cards made for Leroy. He said to us, "Look, fellows, I'm kind of disappointed about what's going on. A few musicians have complained to the union that I'm pimping the kids, saying I'm making money off y'all. All I'm trying to do is preserve this music, and give you something to keep you out of trouble. My hands are tied, and I can't be seen with you. They're talking about fining me, so I'm going to have to lay out." It hurt Mr. Barker that people would be so insecure.

From that point, Charles and Lucien's father, Charles Barbarin Sr., took over the band in a roundabout way. People would still call Mr. Barker, but Mr. Barbarin was coordinating things.

It was Danny Barker's influence, and his vision of preserving the music, that formed my opinions. He would give us reasons for what we were doing, sort of musical history lessons. I was keen enough to understand what he was saying. When you get Japanese people coming to hear the band, and writers coming in, and people from New York sending boxes of instruments, you had to realize that what he was doing was really important. He would nominate different ones amongst us to talk to documentary makers and tell us, "Come with your shoes shined, wear your black and white, look clean." So he gave us a sense of individual pride. He gave us something to keep and cherish: that you are somebody, that you are important, and these are the reasons to preserve your heritage, so you can pass it on to the next generation. That was his thing. When you understand and believe what Danny taught us, and begin to live it, it gives you an understanding of why the heritage should be maintained.

I started going to Preservation Hall, and I saw people like Jim Robinson and Billie and De De Pierce and Paul Barnes. I would listen to Papa John Joseph and Willie and Percy Humphrey. Punch Miller lived two blocks from my house—he had attended school with my grandmother. At that time, they were doing that documentary on Punch, Till the Butcher Cut Him Down. *I would come home from school and see the camera crews. When you become involved with these people and they become personal friends, you become part of that force. People like Harold Dejan, Kid Sheik, Albert Walters, Louis Cottrell, Jack Willis, and Teddy Riley—as I go through life, I remember the moments with these people.*

All those guys were like my father. They all had that same pride about themselves. And as time moves on, you find that musicians of today don't have that fraternal approach that those old men had. I'm just glad that I was born when I was, and lifestyles hadn't changed that much.

When you see people coming in—at that time, you didn't have the different magazines we have today, like Gambit *[and]* OffBeat. *That's when you get people whose livelihood depends on the musician's livelihood—they have to get articles in. In the old days Kid Sheik was Kid Sheik—nobody had to write a microscopic critique about it. These people were just living their lives, and the music was genuine. Now, everybody has an opinion about how this one and that one plays, and everything is being lost about the true essence of the music. I hear people going around raving about other people, and I don't want to step on nobody's toes, but they haven't a clue what traditional jazz is about. It's fair for musicians to present their own objectives, and their own approach to the music, and that's part of being a musician—you have to express yourself. But what I see dwindling away, and I try not to become too opinionated, is the past that I cherished and lived in and experienced. I'm not living in the past, but I bring the past along with me. The music has to evolve, and it's going to evolve; you're going to have people playing differently. But when you see all those values and customs that people took a pride in—then you look at brass bands today!*

I came up at a time when I was playing for Knights of Pythias, Oddfellows, all kinds of Masonic lodges. I saw the membership extend for five or six blocks. In later years, as the membership began to dwindle, I saw those blocks diminishing, as lifestyles changed with the emergence of the insurance companies, so it was no longer necessary to belong to an organization. I lived that. I remember how proud I was, how good I felt about wear-

ing a uniform and band cap. My mother would make sure that my shoes were shined. So you bring this tradition with you.

To see all these customs, and all these songs that had structure, just thrown out of the window—you could hear the Onward band coming up the street sounding like a forty-piece band, all playing in harmony, nobody getting in anybody's way. People don't understand: I even know some musicians who say that I'm trashing other musicians, that I think I'm better than somebody else. It kind of makes you wonder what's important to them.

I don't try to judge people, but I wonder if it's worth all the effort. I still try to stay optimistic about the tradition being preserved, even though people are moving in other directions. But when you hear the media based in the city that tends to think that what everybody's doing is what's happening, it causes people to miss the point and to forget what sacrifices other people have made. Everybody still wants to ride on the coattails of Louis Armstrong, still claiming that they're playing traditional jazz or brass band music. I guess they're using brass band instrumentation, but that's all.

I hope people can appreciate what I'm doing, and can understand. Everybody has their own approach, and I guess I have my place.

Joe Torregano, Saxophones and Clarinet

BORN: New Orleans, February 28, 1952

Played with Dejan's Olympia Band, the Young Tuxedo Brass Band, and the Hurricane
Brass Band; currently with Andrew Hall's Society Brass Band

Interviewed at the corner café on Royal and Conti Streets, October 2001

Joe Torregano with the
Hurricane Brass Band, 1980
Photo by Mike Casimir

*I have one brother, Mike, who's pretty well known in New Orleans. Not everybody
knows that there's a third brother, Louis. He does piano, guitar, bass, organ; he's more
involved in church music. My father, Louis Sr., didn't really play—well, he played
a little piano, but just at home. His godfather was Adolphe "Tats" Alexander, and
his grandfather Joseph, who I'm named after, was a trumpet player in brass bands at
the turn of the century. My father was born in 1910. I've never seen a picture of my
grandfather. One of my family had a picture of him playing, but I don't know what
happened to it.*

*So the three of us brothers are active now. My brother Michael and I are both music
teachers in the school system during the day, in addition to being professional musicians.
I have another brother who lives in Texas, called Ray. His last name is Woodson from
my mother's first marriage. He's retired—he was a schoolteacher and policeman. He's
eighteen years older than me.*

*You couldn't help but come to music if you lived in my house. My mother's name is
Anna; she sang in the church choir. She had a philosophy that her sons should be exposed
to music. At the age of four, we all had to take piano lessons.*

48

My first piano teacher's name was Annabel Jones. I studied with her until she died, when I was around eleven years old. I did my first piano recital when I was five—a tune called "Paper Ships" out of the John Thompson book 1. I studied together with my brother Louis; he's five years my senior. Michael is seven years younger. After Miss Jones, I took lessons with Olivia Charlot Cook. She's a traditional piano player, still living—she's in her mid eighties. She also taught Louis and Michael.

When I was about twelve, I quit playing piano and switched to the clarinet. As a child, I suffered from asthma, and doctors will tell you, if you have any kind of respiratory problems, play a wind instrument—it strengthens the lungs. It's the same reason Pete Fountain took up the clarinet.

My brother Louis gave me my first clarinet lesson—he figured it out from the method book. Then I started taking lessons from Mr. Carey Levigne. He played in a lot of local dance bands and taught in schools, teaching violin and all wind instruments. He had a studio called the Crescent City Music Studio, and among the teachers there were Edwin Hampton, who runs the St. Augustine High School band, Lloyd Harris, Laurence Winchester, Wellington McKissey, Miss Cook, and Willie Humphrey. By me having an interest in jazz, Mr. Levigne talked to Mr. Humphrey, and he agreed to work with me after my regular lessons.

That would be around 1964 until 1967—I studied with Willie all that time. I knew who Willie was, because I went to Craig School on St. Claude, in the Tremé. The original Caldonia bar was in the neighborhood, and I saw jazz funerals several times a week. On Saturdays, my father would bring me out to see jazz funerals, and on Sundays to see the social club parades. So being in contact with Mr. Humphrey wasn't a culture shock. But contrary to what you might think, Willie worked with me on technical exercises more than he did on jazz. He had played in the navy band, and he got me to bring Sousa march books that we were using at school.

He always told me that the technique was just as important as anything else. A lot of my technical skills originate from him and Mr. Levigne. People sometimes tell me I have a lot of technique, and I guess that's true, because I majored in music—I was first at school at Bell Junior High, and the musical director was Donald Richardson, and then to John McDonough Senior High, which is right across from the musician's union on Esplanade.

Mr. Levigne and Mr. Humphrey encouraged me to listen to records and to pick up ideas and melodies from them. Mr. Levigne brought in transcriptions that he made of Benny Goodman solos; I would sit and read those when we had extra time on Saturdays.

I listened to every clarinet player I could find. My favorites from the old school include Omer Simeon, Willie Humphrey, Cornbread Thomas—I don't think there's a clarinet player I don't like.

The first professional job I did, Cornbread was there. I told him, "Well, I've got some of your records at home." He said, "It's nice to see young musicians coming up. It may be your first job, but don't worry—there'll be many more, I'm sure of that."

My first gig was with the Doc Paulin band, like everyone else who wanted to get started. I really wasn't expecting to get paid, but somebody didn't show up, so I got eight dollars for a two-hour parade for the Zulu social club, from one of the churches in the neighborhood. At the end of the job, Doc gave me the eight dollars and told me to be sure and leave my phone number because he would have more work for me.

I stayed with Doc for about a year, and then I met Gregg Stafford—he's a year younger than me. At that time, he was playing with the Fairview band. He told me about that band when he saw that I was interested in the tradition, too. So he got me to come over there, and we rehearsed at Leroy Jones's garage every Monday night, at 1316 St. Denis Street.

It was a big group at that time—we must have had about twenty-three kids. In the original band we had five clarinet players.

We didn't read in rehearsals. I think Danny Barker maybe wrote tunes down for Leroy, and we just picked things up by ear. And by Gregg and I having been with Doc Paulin, we knew a couple of more tunes, which gave us an advantage. Tuba Fats Lacen came in, and a trombone player called Michael Myers, who unfortunately died in a tragic accident in 1976. Donald Gaspard and Branford Marsalis were among the clarinet players at one time. He was a lot more serious than most of those guys. Wynton Marsalis played trumpet with us for a while.

It was a good experience. I think we played together for about ten months, and then we started to get a lot of complaints from professional musicians about people hiring us—if we wanted to play we'd have to join the union. Danny was against us joining the union: I don't know if he felt that some of us weren't ready. He didn't go into detail or explain it to us. I remember, one particular time, he got upset because Greg and I sat in with Andrew Morgan's Young Tuxedo band at the Jazz Fest. It was like, "Those people don't really want you. They're trying to break the band up, but you're over there playing with them anyway."

What happened after that, I left the band and joined the union when I was twenty. The writing was on the wall, and the band was going to break up anyway. I didn't have any guarantees of work or anything, but it happened that Harold Dejan knew that Danny was getting union pressure. He told me, "If you join the union, call me." So he started to use me as an alternative when Emanuel Paul would be out with the Kid Thomas band. This was in 1972. After about two jobs, Harold took me on one side and said, "Do you think you could get away from school for about two weeks, next month?" My first tour of Europe, and I was only twenty years old.

Just before that trip, Andrew Morgan died, and Herman Sherman took over his band. They asked me to join them. So I was in the Olympia and the Young Tuxedo at the same time, which was the best of both worlds.

We went over in November, and our first stop was London. This particular band was Harold, Paul Crawford, myself, Milton Batiste, Nowell Glass, Andrew Jefferson, Anderson Minor was the grand marshal, and Irving Eisen played tuba—he was originally from St. Louis and was playing on Bourbon Street at Your Father's Moustache at the time. Alan Jaffe recommended him because Coby Brown couldn't make it. It was a two-week trip—London, Paris, Copenhagen, Amsterdam.

Now, the Hurricane band started after Danny organized the second Fairview band. Michael White was in it; the Mimms brothers and Daryl Adams were there. Then Leroy ventured out on his own and started the Hurricane band. That band made one album, for Jules Cahn—he produced that album. He was a photographer; he died around five years ago. Gregg Stafford and I are actually on the album, but you don't see our last names—it says Joseph Charles and Gregory Vaughan. It was so the union couldn't say anything about us being on a nonunion recording. The song "Leroy Special" wasn't written by Leroy Jones, as most people assume. It was by Leroy Robinet, but he wrote it for Leroy Jones.

The band didn't last that long, the fantasy of playing on the street; we were all maturing, and Leroy went off to college at Loyola. We were at that age when we were spreading out, going to school. After about two years, we started to go our separate ways. Herman Sherman was running the Young Tuxedo by then, and he asked me to put pressure on Gregg Stafford to join the union because he needed a dependable trumpet player.

Only a handful of us were really dedicated to traditional music. I've been teaching in the school system for twenty-seven years, and I feel we don't pass down enough of our traditions to our kids anymore. Almost the whole Creole tradition is going, the language and everything—it's very, very rare.

The Eureka Brass Band was the greatest brass band I heard when I was a kid on the way up. I've heard—whether it's true I don't know—that the reason that band died out was because they wouldn't let younger guys in. They got up in age, they couldn't handle the parades anymore, and so they stopped taking them. You couldn't blame them for taking it easy; they'd paid their dues, and they blazed a trail for me and Gregg and Leroy and all these guys to follow.

Anyway, after the Hurricane band, I was regular with the Young Tuxedo. Herman Sherman was a taskmaster—not fierce, not brutal, but he had certain disciplines that *he wanted met. At the same time, he looked at Gregg and I like his own sons. He made me assistant leader before I had been in the band a year. We had Walter Payton on tuba, Frank Naundorf on trombone, Reginald Koeller, Fernandez [Albert Walters], Gregg and John Simmons on trumpets. Teddy Riley would come and go; later on we had Jack Willis for a long time, Emile Knox on bass drum, Lawrence Trotter on snare drum. Herman was always ready to listen to ideas for marketing the band. Gregg and I helped him—we had pictures made, we helped book jobs, took the pressure off him a bit.*

We did the Hollywood Bowl, the Berlin Jazz Festival, we went to Chicago. Herman called the tunes. He and Ernest ["Doc"] Watson would get some great riffs going—they'd worked together in the Groovy Boys.

I got my degree in music education in 1975, and I went back to Bell Junior High, which I had attended as a student. I move around a lot—there weren't any permanent jobs back then.

Technically, I'm still in the Young Tuxedo—I've been in the band for twenty-nine years now. Herman passed away in 1984, and a lot of people thought that, having been assistant leader of the band, I should have been the next one to take it on. But for whatever reason, Gregg Stafford took over, and that's all I'm going to say about that. You talk to different members of the band, you'll have different stories about what they thought and why, but I try to stay out of that. It's a shame that we haven't played much for the last six or seven years. Basically, you see the band at Jazz and Heritage Festival, maybe one or two other special events during a year. So it's not totally dead, but it's kind of mothballed.

I left the Olympia band after eight years—that was my own decision. I had recently married, there were kids on the way, and I had my music teaching. That was in about 1981. Doc Watson took my place in the Olympia. I was working for Bob French, and we were getting a lot of work at different clubs on Bourbon Street.

I did the One Mo' Time *show a couple of times. Then, in 1989, I started my police career. My oldest brother was a police officer, and one of my best friends also. I joined the resource division of the police department. We are all volunteers. We have the same training, police academy and all. I'm required to do twenty-four hours' service every month. I love it—not as much as playing music, but I do love it. I've been on stage with some of the greatest musicians of all time, and the police work is like my way of saying thank you to New Orleans.*

I'm running my own four-piece band now with my brother Michael, and I play with the eight-piece Creole band Eh, La-Bas. We do some old Creole songs, some New Orleans, R&B. We're just about to do a new CD, and we've just come back from touring in Britain—seventeen one-nighters and twenty-eight hundred miles in twenty days. It was rough!

If I hadn't been born in New Orleans, I probably wouldn't have become a musician. I don't think there's another town in America, or probably the world, where you would get this much exposure to music at an early age. Every kid in my music classes has a relative who plays music. They all want to be involved.

You may be surprised to hear this, but I'm not like some of the other musicians you've interviewed—they'll make it seem like music is their life. Even though my life is music, because I teach it and I play it and I love it, it's not my total life. I've never let music come between me and my family or between me and the police department. Whatever I do at school or on the bandstand stays there when I walk away. I enjoy what I do, and I'm constantly reminding other musicians that we're blessed to be able to do what we love and get paid for it. We're the luckiest motherfuckers in the world!

Harry Sterling, Guitar

BORN: New Orleans, March 18, 1958

Danny Barker's only guitar pupil; played tuba with the Fairview Baptist Church Brass Band; currently plays guitar with Big Al Carson's Blues Masters

Interviewed at 3621 Burgundy Street, October 2002

Photo by Barry Martyn

My mother and father were Laura and Harrison Sterling. I am the last of five children. None of the others are musicians. Originally, I had planned to be a meteorologist. When Hurricane Betsy hit New Orleans in 1965, it was fascinating to me that something like that could rock my parent's house. Watching the news, they showed radar pictures, although they were pretty crude back then. I got interested in the weather and how it moved. I would make makeshift maps of the United States, and when the weather came on TV, I would mark down what was going on. I was seven years old then.

When I was in elementary school, getting ready to go to junior high—this would be around the age of twelve—I was at my cousin's house. We were playing ball in his front yard, and I heard the sound of a banjo—the sound just caught my attention. I was looking round and missing the ball. I said, "What's that noise behind me?" He said, "That's Cousin Danny"—that's what he called him. I said, "We don't have no cousin called Danny, not that I know of."

Anyway, he brought me over there to meet him. I was fascinated at the way his fingers moved up and down the neck—he had switched to guitar by then. I was mesmerized. He was practicing, and he and Miss Louise were getting ready to rehearse. She was in the kitchen cooking. When we got to the back door, this big raspy voice comes out of the house, and there's this lady standing there.

I had never heard a woman with a voice that deep before, so she kind of scared me. She called, "Danny, Ray and his cousin Harry are here." So we go in the front and we sit down. I'm not saying anything—Ray's doing all the talking. I'm just looking at Danny and thinking, "I've got to do that."

Two days before my twelfth birthday, it had been on my mind for about a week. I knew I had to go back around there and talk to this man about learning the guitar. I

mustered up enough courage to go into their yard and stand at the back door. And this scary woman with this big raspy voice called, "Danny, it's Ray's cousin Harry." She had remembered my name!

He said, "What can I do for you?" I said, "I want to talk to you." So we went into the front room, and I asked where his guitar was. He said, "It's in the back. What can I do for you?" And I told him I wanted to learn to play. He said, "Are you sure you want to?" I said, "Oh yeah." It was fixed in my mind. He asked me if I owned a guitar. I said I didn't, my parents couldn't afford one. He kind of put his head down, and he told me that the guitar was a very wonderful instrument, but it takes a lot of practice and a lot of patience to learn. He explained about how a guitar was strung and what the frets were for. I was absorbing all of it, and I had a smile on my face.

Then he shouts, "Louise! Make this boy a sandwich!"

I'm like, "I don't want a sandwich. I want to learn to play the guitar." Anyway, Miss Louise comes out the back with this sandwich—ham and cheese, on toast, lettuce, and tomato, pickles, potato chips, and a Coke!

I thought, "Well, I can't insult these people by not eating it." While I'm eating the sandwich, Danny Barker comes out the back with this little acoustic guitar and this chord book with fingering charts in it. He explained as well as he could that each dot represents your finger, and the strings go down, and the frets go across.

He put my fingers on the guitar, and it sounded terrible. He asked me if my parents were home. I told him my mother was home, but my father was out at the church. He asked me where I lived, and I told him right around the corner, on St. Denis, 1265, and I gave him my phone number. Leroy Jones lived just down the street from me. By now, my finger was beginning to hurt terribly, but I didn't care.

Afterwards, I was walking down the street, wondering how I was going to explain to my mother how come I had this guitar. I went in the house, and she gave me this "report-card day" look: "What is that? Where did you get it?" I told her I had got it from Danny Barker, and she said, "What? Blue Lou Barker's husband?" I said, "Who's Blue Lou Barker?" Then I found out that was Miss Louise with the raspy voice.

I told her, "Mr. Barker says for you to call him." So she talked to him on the phone. He said, "I'm not charging you a cent. You can't afford a guitar, and I understand. I have quite a few of them, so this one won't be missed. I'm going to teach your boy to play, keep his mind occupied and keep him off the streets."

This was basically his main premise—he didn't want me hanging out on the corner. But hanging out on the corner wasn't part of my parent's plan for me anyway. Six o'clock was dinner. You had to be inside, washed up, and ready to sit down and eat. My mother said to me, "I'm not going to tell you when to practice. You're on your own. Go get your lessons from Mr. Barker. If this is what you choose to do, that's OK." But I had made that choice the first day I saw Danny Barker play.

They had to tell me to stop practicing: "Boy, put that guitar up and go to bed. It's time to give it a rest." I was just trying to get a sound on the guitar that was clear. After about two weeks, I got the first chord to sound like it should. Danny was really pleased about that. So then he started showing me more chords, and the more difficult they got, the more my fingers hurt. I can't tell you—I put the guitar down for one day, and when I went to pick it up, it was agony. I complained about the pain, but Mr. Barker told me that this comes with the territory. If you play the trumpet, your lips are going to hurt; if you play drums, you're gonna get cramps in your wrists.

Danny was fabulous to me—he never raised his voice. When it came down to him making a point about something, he was very, very stern about doing the right thing. He was like a second father. I spent a lot of time by his house, to learn, and what he taught me, the things he said, he meant. He said that being a musician is a terrible thing—there will be days that you're not going to eat, days that you're not gonna work, days that people won't want to hear you play. I understood that sometimes you might starve. But every time I went by his house, he would ask if I was sure I wanted to be a musician. After about two and a half years, he stopped asking me.

I was going to his house practically every day, just to learn something new. Then he told me I didn't need to come every day—I could come once a week. I had to learn to sing and play a particular song for him, and then he would give me another song to learn. I remember learning "The Saints," "This Little Light of Mine," "Down by the Riverside"—the traditional New Orleans songs, with basic chord changes. Then one day I went to get my lesson, and he was playing "Eh la Bas." I fell in love with that song. I asked him what language it was, and he told me it was French. He sang and played it again, and I stopped him and said, "How do you change chords so quickly?" He looked at me and said, "How old are you, Harry?" I told him I was thirteen.

He said, "I've been playing the guitar a lot longer than you've been around. After a while, you memorize the neck of the guitar. You'll learn to play without looking. That's gonna come." He said, "Grab that guitar." It was a Gibson Super 400, something I knew nothing about. It was too big for me—if I held the neck, my arms was too short to reach the body. We started playing "The Saints" in F. I had just mastered the chord of F—it's difficult to play: you have to hold down two strings with one finger. He asked me to sing it, and I did.

Then he asked me if I had played in church, and I told him no. I said that there was a program coming up, and I was going to ask my parents if it was OK to perform. I asked my mom if I could play, but she told me that they were very strict, and if you weren't

baptized, you couldn't participate. So, being a kid, I said, "OK, I still want to do it anyway." So we went to the pastor of the church, and he said, "Sure, you can play. What are
you going to play?" I said, "This Little Light of Mine."

So they called my name—and I didn't have no strap! I had to grab a chair, throw
my leg on the chair, and throw the guitar on my lap. Members of the choir said, "He
looks just like Glen Campbell." I had my head down; I was playing and I was terrified.
The church is packed with maybe a hundred people—and I actually played each chord
without looking. It was scary.

Without realizing it, I had been watching TV in my room when I was practicing.
I had got used to glancing at the chord book and the guitar without having to move my
head. Eventually, I could watch TV without having to look to see where I'm at. Sometimes now, when I'm playing at the Funky Pirate, I'll be watching the ball game on
the television at the front while I'm playing—people think I'm just gazing into the distance.

In 1972, Danny told me he was starting a community band. I said I'd like to be part of
it, but they didn't need a guitar player. They gathered in my cousin's grandmother's
den: Danny Barker, Ernie Cagnolatti, Ayward Johnson, Charles Barbarin Sr., Joe Torregano—the list just went on and on. Charles Barbarin the younger, his brother Lucien,
Leroy Jones, Raymond "Puppy" Johnson, Derek Cagnolatti, Roy Paisant on trombone,
Steven Parker the tuba player (big tall cat), Thomas and Gene Mimms. Thomas is a
doctor now; Gene is a teacher in Atlanta. He still plays from time to time—fabulous soprano sax player. Herlin Riley, he's playing drums with Wynton Marsalis now. Herlin
came into the Funky Pirate one night, and I didn't know him. I hadn't seen him since
1975, when he was playing trumpet.

So Danny put this band together, and I wanted to play so bad. I'm listening to them
all—they had all started playing years before me, and I had come to it late. Then they
started calling the names of the people who were going to be in the band. They called my
name, to play the banjo. They told me, "This banjo has six strings, so you'll be able to
play it." So I had black pants, white shirt, and a parade cap. The Jazz Fest was about
to come up, and we played at Jazz Fest when it was in Congo Square. With Danny being
the one that put the band together, he was playing the banjo. So I carried the band's sign,
which I was more than happy to do. I did that for a good while with the Fairview band.

Then came the day I did play the banjo with the band. They took a picture outside
Fairview Church—Gene and Thomas on one side, me on the other, Greg, Steve, Leroy,
Lucien, Raymond. When you look at the picture, Gene Mimms and me look like twins.

It got to the point where my musical siblings—sort of sibling rivalry—didn't want a
banjo in the band. I wasn't really that good a player—these guys were taking solos, and

I'm still struggling just to play basic chords. I wanted to play with the Fairview band, but my name was already ex—Fairview band—history.

In the junior high school, I wanted to play something else. I really wanted to learn the saxophone, but the band director put me on tuba. It gave me an opportunity to learn different things, and the late, great Raymond Myers, the gospel maestro, was at high school with me, and he taught me how to play tuba. After about a month, I could play OK.

When I got to the point when I thought I could play OK, I went round the corner to Mr. Barker's house, and he gave me every brass band album he had. By that time, I was going to Houston's for music, on Claiborne next door to the Louisiana Funeral Home. I learned the notes on guitar first and transferred that to the tuba. My favorite tuba player was Wilbert Tillman on records—I tried to emulate him.

By then the Fairview band had become a huge brass band, with three tubas—Anthony Lacen, Steve Parker, and myself. This was just before the start of Leroy Jones and the Hurricane Brass Band. We did this performance out at Chalmette, with four tubas in the band. We were all playing great. Danny came to the back and signaled me to stop playing. Then he said, "Play." After the performance, he said to me, "You have the fattest sound I've ever heard on tuba."

We didn't read at rehearsal. Leroy practiced every day, and we would practice at his house. I had learned most of the tunes from the albums I had borrowed from Danny.

Then Danny told me he was going to be out of town too much to give me lessons, and I had to get another teacher. As time went on, I started venturing away from the traditional New Orleans jazz, because there was so much more out there.

I went to lessons with Mr. Frank Murray at Houston's. I was a little bit arrogant when I went in—I really didn't want to be there. Mr. Murray said, "Play me something," and I did. He said, "Who was your teacher?" and I told him. Then he sort of sat for about five minutes with his head in his hands. Then he said, "You sound like shit, but when you leave here, you'll be a very good guitarist. A reading musician is a working musician." I went to lessons with him for three and a half years, every Saturday at exactly twelve o'clock. It was good discipline—he drove me nuts. By knowing the bass clef, I played the bass charts with Kid Johnson's big band.

I first met Al Carson when I was fourteen years old. I was playing at a friend's wedding, and they had a nun singing a pop version of the Lord's Prayer—I sang the middle part, because they couldn't quite get it. Afterwards, at the reception, at the Bricklayer's Hall on Galvez Street, I was the first one out of the car—all of us looking real cool in our suits. I said, "Hey, listen, they're doing 'Mighty Mighty' by Earth, Wind and Fire."

I ran up to the door and said, "Hey! They got this big dude on the bandstand, sound just like the record." I didn't know him, but I was mesmerized. In the front of the Bricklayer's Hall, there was a champagne fountain. We got some cups, I went to get the drinks—I'm the biggest of my group. Who should be standing up there but Big Al Carson. He says, "Hey, boy! Put that champagne down, you got no business drinking that! I'll tell your momma on you!" I remembered him for years.

Four years later, I was applying for a scholarship at Xavier University. We hadn't had the results, and I went up there to see what was going on, just as they were having a concert band rehearsal. I looked to my left, and Big Al was playing tuba. I went over there, and said, "How you doing? Remember about four years ago, you played with a band called Better Half? You played at Irwin Johnson's wedding at the Bricklayer's Hall." He said, "Yeah, I remember that." I said, "Remember that kid you told to put the champagne down?" He said, "Was that your little brother?" I said, "No, that was me." We became the best of friends. We didn't start playing together until around 1980.

We got together to rehearse and record some songs I had written when I was in the hospital for a month. He sang lead, and three of us sang backing. Al named the band Sterlyn Silver. We recorded some stuff, but we didn't do anything with it, because we didn't have any money, and Al was on the road with One Mo' Time. He's got about three and a half octaves, and all in tune—he's disgusting!

The Fairview band basically broke up because everyone was getting older and getting into other musical things. So then Danny Barker started the Younger Fairview band and brought in Michael White and myself. I was still in college, and so was Michael. That's when we met Eddie Bo Parish, Efrem Towns, Gerry Anderson, William Smith on trumpet, Curtis Walker on trombone, Dwight Johnson on bass drum, Byron Washington on snare. We would play traditional tunes in the French Quarter for tips.

Danny sent us to Kentucky to play at a horse auction—it was great. We would play at the plantations on River Road and wedding receptions and stuff. I was getting really weary of the tuba. Then they had Wolf—Keith Anderson—come in and play tuba. By now they had changed the name to the Charlie Barbarin Memorial Jazz Band. But by then I had quit—I was gigging. They used to come to get me to do brass band gigs in the morning, when I hadn't got to bed until 4:00 A.M. They would come in my yard and play, shouting, "Come on, Big H! We got to go to work." The years with those guys were great, but I wanted to concentrate on my guitar playing—by then I was starting to play classical music.

I've now been working with Big Al Carson at the Funky Pirate on Bourbon Street for eight years, and it doesn't look like the job is likely to finish any time soon. Usually on Bourbon Street bands last a year, maybe two, then they change the policy or something.

HARRY STERLING, GUITAR   59

We figured we'd just do the gig, take the money, and run. Two years became three, three became five, five wound up being eight. It's never been about the money, but when you get older, you have responsibilities. And as Al says, he's never missed a meal in his life, and he doesn't want to start now! And at this time in my life, I'm not ready to get up in the morning to punch somebody's clock. I'd rather be at the Funky Pirate, 727 Bourbon Street, sitting on my butt, playing the blues behind Big Al Carson.

Tad Jones, Jazz Writer and Historian

BORN: New Orleans, September 19, 1952

Interviewed at Hogan Jazz Archive, Tulane University, November 2002

I've been going to parades since about 1969. I met Jules Cahn that way. I was doing research on the Mardi Gras Indians, and Jules was very involved with that; he knew a great deal about the various tribes. He was a great cultural voyeur—always at the parades on Sundays, with his camera. He didn't leave any books or memoirs—I wish he had—but he did leave us his photographs, and they're at the Historic New Orleans Collection.

He lived on Versailles, and I lived on Belfast Street, so we were only six blocks away from each other. Often we'd go to parades together. He had very broad tastes, and he liked a lot of different people.

Jules was a friend of Danny Barker's, and I'm sure he knew the musicians from the Fairview band. He told me about the Hurricane Brass Band when it started, and we went to hear them a couple of times. They were young and inexperienced; it was young, raw, energetic. They weren't trying to do anything new and different—they had come up with Danny, so they were trying to stick to the old traditions. The musicians from that band were probably the last influence from Danny's era. The cutoff is really in the eighties, with the Rebirth and Dirty Dozen; by that stage, the tradition had really gone.

At some point, Jules said, out of the goodness of his heart (he was personally wealthy, owned Dixie Lumber Mill and a lot of property in the French Quarter), "I'd like to make a record of the Hurricane band, but I don't want to spend a lot of money on a fancy studio."

I told him I had a reel-to-reel tape recorder; it was stereo, a good solid machine. We went out to his brother's house, out on Lakeview. We had food and drinks, and we set the band up in a corner and balanced the sound. We started in the afternoon. I'd switch on the tape, point at them, and shout, "Take One!" That was the first time I'd done anything like that. After about three hours, we'd recorded the whole album. I think we issued everything from the session. It was to help promote the band at the time. I'm sure they didn't press more than a thousand copies. I remember thinking that the test pressing sounded pretty good, considering it had been done in someone's house, on a home tape recorder.

Leroy Jones and His Hurricane Marching Brass Band of New Orleans
RECORDED MARCH 1 AND 2, 1975

Personnel   Charles Barbarin Jr., bass drum. Joseph Charles [Torregano], clarinet. Leroy Jones Jr., trumpet and leader. Darryl Adams, alto saxophone. Lucien Barbarin, trombone. Michael Johnson, trombone. Anthony Lacen, sousaphone. Henry Freeman, tenor saxophone. Gregory Davis, trumpet. Gregory Vaughn [Gregg Stafford], trumpet. Raymond Johnson Jr., snare drum.

Titles   "Little Liza Jane," "Bourbon Street Parade," "Leroy's Special," "Oh, Didn't He Ramble," "Closer Walk with Thee," "The Saints Go Marching In," "Nearer My God to Thee," "Joe Avery's Tune," "The Battle Hymn of the Republic," "Olympia Special."

BAND CALL

Dirty Dozen Brass Band

A Note on the Tremé and Its Music

Claude Tremé created the oldest faubourg (suburb) in New Orleans around 1812. Originally the home of many skilled artisan gens de couleur libre (free people of color), the area still has some of the most distinctive and elegant architecture in the city.

Its geographical boundaries seem to be a matter of opinion. In *Backbeat: Earl Palmer's Story,* Tony Scherman cites a 1980 architectural study as indicating that "the Tremé extends from North Rampart to North Broad Streets, and from Canal Street to St. Bernard Avenue," but he goes on to say, "Most people . . . consider it much smaller: the thirty block area extending on one side from Rampart to North Claiborne, on the other from Orleans to Esplanade."[15] Austin Leslie, interviewed for the Tremé Oral History Project, said, "The Tremé is from Lafitte to Esplanade, down Claiborne, and North Rampart to St. Peter." Norman Smith, another interviewee for that project, indicated the neighborhood runs "from Galvez to Burgundy, from Lafitte to St. Bernard. In later years, the boundaries have been extended to Elysian Fields."[16]

What most people would regard as the area's economic decline during the last century coincided with a cultural richness and identity, particularly in the amount of music that emanated from the Tremé and the appreciative enthusiasm that supported it. Recollecting the mid-1950s, Ernest "Doc" Watson recalled, "I would see the older guys playing on the street. . . . That music was very popular in the Tremé section—the people would do these little street dances, and so forth. Whenever we played in the Tremé section, Little Millett would wait until around midnight, and start calling those old Dixieland numbers. You had to play that stuff down there."[17] Milton Batiste, recalling working in "the Sixth Ward," remembered, "They had plenty of nightclubs there: the High Hat, the Caldonia and the other dance halls. . . . This was the very epitome of where blues and jazz actually was born."[18]

William Smith explains that the love of music helped create a strong sense of community in the neighborhood: "It's like—this is a high crime city, usually I lock my car when I go anywhere. But I can go in the Tremé and leave it unlocked, with the tuba on the seat, and my horn on the hood, and they're not going to touch it. Because that would stop the band from playing."[19]

Older residents look back to a time of order and cultural stability, when goats pulled little carts to the icehouse to keep the beer cold, where disagreements were resolved by fisticuffs on Nanny Goat Square rather than by shootings, and Sunday afternoons were spent making music for the sheer fun of the thing. As Norman Smith recalled,

I lived on North Robertson—we had a unique neighborhood, and many of the people were very talented. My earliest memories of music in Tremé took place right in my backyard. The music was very unique—there were lots of traditional hymns. There were not many singers around then, but a lot of people who played instruments.

Some of the Batiste family lived on St. Philip Street. The family was very musically inclined, and on a Sunday after church, when everybody had cooked their dinner and what have you, they would get in the backyard, and they'd make a big crock of Sangria, and they would put up a card table. Some people would play cards, and the Batiste family would get out their makeshift instruments and play music. There was the washboard, the comb and paper. My mother had a beautiful porcelain-topped table, and the guy that was supposed to be the drummer was playing on the table with two forks. One day we were having so much fun in the yard, and the adults were drinking the Sangria and the Eagle beer. My mother looked down, and all round the corner of the table the forks had chipped the porcelain off. She broke the party up that day.[20]

Chef Austin Leslie, a long-term Tremé resident, was for many years the proprietor of Chez Helene restaurant at 932 North Claiborne. Trade and the neighborhood went down together. In 1996, he was running the New Orleans restaurant in Copenhagen, Denmark. After a couple of years, he returned to the States and went to work in Oakland, California. Fortunately for New Orleans, that didn't work out, and in November 2002, he was back, using his considerable culinary skills at Jacques Imo's on Oak Street. It seemed to be going well—they don't take reservations for parties of less than five. He recalled his younger days in the Tremé:

I was born in the Seventh Ward, but I came to the Lafitte projects when I was in third grade. I went to Craig School. There was a teacher there called Miss Morton. She was a music teacher, and she put out people like John Fernandez, who was a trumpet player—he was one of my classmates. I can remember when Fats Domino and them used to play back of the Caldonia, in the Tremé section, right at St. Claude and St. Philip.

They had a lot of second lines going through then. Years ago, they had the Center Club on Dumaine between Villere and Marais. A lot of stuff used to go on in there. You had people like Rip Roberts—he used to bring different entertainers down. I can remember Ray Charles coming in there years ago. Dooky Chase Sr., the old man, he would parade with the Square Deals. Like the parades that are going on now, like the youngsters have different parades throughout the year. They'd go by Rampart Street and get their clothes, all the different colors, with the sashes and all. It was good times in New Orleans then. I've been around it so long I feel like my feet hurt with that tar and asphalt, trying to catch up with those bands. Now I just look at them. History excites me—it's like being in this area here, you know? I was born and raised here.

I enjoy music—I like old jazz, and I remember the music from the sanctified churches. In the Tremé, you were right in the thick of it. I lived on 1854 North Miro. The drummer Earl Palmer, he lived right on the edge of the Tremé, and the guitar player Walter "Papoose" Nelson. He was very young, but he played with Fats Domino. I was always connected around music.

I remember the vegetable man coming through the Tremé to the French market—back then, he would push a small wagon to carry the vegetables. On Fridays, he would sell seafood from the wagon, which was against the law. The cops would come and shake him down; if he couldn't pay them off, they'd take his seafood.

My music was more like, any time someone died, they would have a second line, so we'd follow that. They had a lot of clubs—the Jolly Bunch, the Square Deals, and so forth, social and pleasure clubs.[21]

The social problems that afflict the Tremé today are pretty well spread throughout the neighborhoods of the city. Recent years have seen a school child shot to death for possession of his bike, a crack dealer burned alive in the street during a turf war, and too many drive-by shootings to count. In 1962, Dejan's Olympia Brass Band was the only one that dared venture into the Tremé for the funeral of guitarist Papoose Nelson. The other bands were too scared. It's the kind of crime that comes from lack of opportunity and loss of cultural identity. These problems don't start in the Tremé, but that's where some of them end up.

The identity of the area is not only threatened by the social malaise of the inner city. In the late sixties, fourteen blocks were demolished to make the space that became Armstrong Park, and the I-10 expressway was extended over Claiborne Avenue, thus obliterating a tree-shaded meeting place and parade route and forcing a lot of people to move somewhere else. Whether the location of these projects was racially motivated (as many people believe) or merely the kind of ill-considered decision that seemed to characterize most urban planning at the time, the effect was not beneficial to the community. As Norman Smith observed,

> I was living in Tremé when we happened to see the destruction of all of the families that were living where current-day Armstrong Park is. There was a number of very historic landmarks within the confines of that area that have been erased, and it's so unfortunate because many of the families go all the way back to the days of slavery. When those families were dispersed, their whole history was wiped out. It was tragic—these were proud people, they were very enlightened in the cultural aesthetics of living. When they were uprooted and placed in housing developments, it was a devastating blow.[22]

Drummer Benny Jones, who had married into the legendary Batiste family, belonged to a number of social and pleasure clubs, which were gaining strength in the late seventies. Many of the clubs approached Benny to supply bands for second line parades, and he looked around for musicians. Edgar Smith explains,

> The Majestic Brass Band started in 1977 as an offshoot of Doc Paulin's band; before that we were taking jobs as the Doc Paulin Band Part Two. The Majestic had a number two band, called the Voodoo Band. They had Kirk and Charles Joseph, Greg Davis, Roger Lewis and Efrem Towns.
>
> Then Benny Jones got our second band musicians and started to practice with them. He came to Flo [Floyd Anckle, the Majestic bandleader] and said, "I need some musicians." Flo told him, "Take those boys. Take the Voodoo Band, call it what you want."[23]

The name Benny chose was the Original Sixth Ward Dirty Dozen Brass Band.

Gregory "Blodie" Davis, Trumpet

BORN: New Orleans, January 30, 1957

Played with the Hurricane Brass Band and briefly with the Majestic Brass Band; leader of the Dirty Dozen Brass Band

Interviewed at the offices of Festival Productions on Camp Street, October 2002

I've lived most of my life here in New Orleans. For a brief period in the sixties, the family moved out to Los Angeles, but that was only for about a year and a half. Fortunately, we came back to New Orleans.

My family's not particularly large: I have three brothers and one sister. I have one brother who plays keyboards in the church, but I'm the only one who has made music my primary source of income. I had an older brother who went to summer music camp. He was more into the sports side of it, and when he would leave to go to camp, he wouldn't bring his instrument—he'd leave it at home. I'd sneak it out and play. It was a baritone horn.

I was in the seventh grade, at the age of twelve, just fooling round with the horn, teaching myself. After that summer, when school opened, I enrolled in the music class. At that time, I went to Andrew J. Bell school. After three years there, I went on to St. Augustine. That's when I met Leroy Jones. My original intent was to play drums. There were maybe twenty other kids in the class that wanted to play drums, and maybe two drums. So I just didn't see a future in that. The instructor offered me a French horn, but I thought the case was kind of ugly; I didn't want to carry it on the bus. The next pretty-looking case that he had was the one for a cornet. So at thirteen, I ended up playing cornet in the junior high school band.

My track went like this: in the beginning, I was in the school marching band. From that point, I started playing with some of the rhythm and blues and funk bands here in New Orleans. Friends would form a band, and we'd play. I didn't really have any influences; I was just playing the trumpet in the band. Just learning how to play some music, without any particular direction. I spent some time with Jean Knight, who had a hit record with "Mr. Big Stuff" in the seventies.

Then I went on to high school, where I became friends with Leroy Jones. He had been under Danny Barker's tutelage with the Fairview Baptist Church band. Then he went on to form the Hurricane Brass Band, and he asked me to join it.

As he progressed on his instrument, playing jazz and all, he got too busy to maintain the Hurricane band. He was playing on Bourbon Street and doing other things. Myself and some of the others started another brass band, which we called the Tor-

nado. That lasted a couple of months. Money problems—stuff was just happening that shouldn't. So we moved on and started another unit, which ended up being the Dirty Dozen.

That's where my association with Danny Barker really came about. It was through his teaching of Leroy and the others I could trace my musical line back to him. With the Dirty Dozen, we featured Danny on The New Orleans Album.

When the group started, there was no work. Nobody was really hiring brass bands. In the mid to late seventies, there wasn't enough to keep the Hurricane band working, and that's what had caused Leroy to move on—there was more of an opportunity for him to play and earn money on Bourbon Street at that time. So when we started the Dozen, it was meant to be a rehearsal group more than anything else, because there wasn't any work going around.

The original group was myself, Kirk and Charles Joseph. Tuba Fats used to come to the rehearsals, but when we started playing things other than just traditional music, Tuba didn't want to do that. Roger Lewis was actually working with Fats Domino when we got the band started. He came along right at the end of the Tornado band; he came out to play a parade with us. And then he came with us in the Dirty Dozen. We had another cornet player named Cyrille Salvant (he's dead now), and Andrew "Big Daddy" Green and Benny Jones played drums.

In the beginning, there was a lot of rehearsal going on, so several people were in and out. We started to develop a repertoire. Then we knew who the band was going to be. There was me, Efrem Towns, Roger Lewis, Kevin Harris on tenor sax, Charles and Kirk Joseph, Jenell Marshall on snare drum, and Benny Jones on bass drum. We were the eight people who took it out on the road.

At the time, I was studying at Loyola University, and Roger and Charles were studying at Southern University with Kidd Jordan. Our influences were rhythm and blues, bebop, post-bebop like John Coltrane, Freddie Hubbard, Art Blakey and the Jazz Messengers. I was listening to Dizzy Gillespie and Charlie Parker and Miles Davis. So we were hearing music coming from everywhere. We recorded the tune "Bongo Beep," which I had heard on a record and brought to the rehearsal. That's how we operated: we weren't working a lot, so in addition to learning traditional New Orleans music, guys would say, "Hey, here's something interesting I just heard. Let's see what we can do with it." At the time, we were just rehearsing, and we were interested in learning the chord progressions and the melodies, that kind of stuff. Whoever brought the songs in, it was their responsibility to bring the charts. We were all free to bring whatever we wanted to rehearsal. We weren't thinking about getting gigs.

The interesting thing about it was, some of us were in school, some of us were newly married, some had jobs and whatever, but no matter what, we rehearsed almost every night. And rehearsals would start at nine o'clock at night and go on until 2:00 A.M. It was just the fun of getting together and playing. This was at a time when disco was happening. All of Bourbon Street had turned disco—there was no live music anywhere. No one was really hiring bands. So the only chance we had to play was at rehearsals. The band was founded on love of music.

The first few gigs that we had as a unit were at a softball game, or birthday party—some of them didn't even pay any money; we just did them because they were a chance for us to play. It was a very localized thing: we were firmly grounded in the Tremé area. On the bass drum, our name was the Original Sixth Ward Dirty Dozen.

As I can recall (and I'm sure if you talk to someone else, you'll get a different story), the band before I got in there would march around on Halloween as some kind of joke, with kazoos and stuff. But then some of the social and pleasure clubs that had been in existence and had gone away wanted to start having a brass band at their picnics and parties, play funerals, or whatever.

Benny Jones, who was in the social and pleasure club scene (he was a part of that world) was asked to put a band together. So he would call us to come out and do those jobs. Once I assumed leadership of the group, I thought it would be better to use the same people as often as I could, because they knew the repertoire that we had rehearsed. That helped to keep it tight.

Our first regular gig was at a place called Daryl's, a small black club in the Seventh Ward. It was happening for us on a Thursday night—it grew into something big. The Glasshouse job started on Monday night and became even bigger than Daryl's. How it happened was this. The Sunday before, we had performed at one of the second line parades—it may have been for the Money Wasters or one of those. The parade ended at the Glasshouse—it can probably comfortably seat about thirty people or something like that. The people who hired us wanted us to play a few more songs after the parade ended. The Glasshouse sold out of everything they had during the hour that we played.

On Monday nights, the social and pleasure clubs would get together and start planning their parades and have something to eat and drink. They asked us to come out and play for them after the meeting. We played, and they sold everything they had again. So then they decided to do it every Monday night. It lasted about seven to eight years. But we went for seven years without missing a Monday. Once we started traveling, it became more difficult to get back for that job. That's how the Rebirth got started: they were hired to substitute for us on Monday nights when we couldn't get there. Eventually, our weekend trips turned into two weeks, three, five- or six-week trips, and it just got impossible.

We had everything going for us. While it was happening, I don't think any of us were really thinking, "OK, we got this in place, let's make it work." It was just a gig, and it was fun to do, and we were playing this supposedly new music. Really, there wasn't anything new about it—we were just taking things that had already been done, just adding a little something to it, changing it a little bit.

But these young dancers were coming out to the gigs in groups. They would challenge us with their dancing, they'd do some steps, and we'd have to say, "OK, now you top this. We'll play something." The next week, we'd have something new for them to try and top what we were doing. It was a competitive kind of thing. So not only did the music change, but the style of second lining and buck jumping changed also, along with what we were doing. Now that I look back on it, I can see the development, whereas when I was in it, I wasn't really paying attention to what was happening.

It's had its ups and downs. One of the reasons the band has lasted so long is because we were able to weather the storms. In the music business nobody's up all the time. But we had enough going on, even when we didn't have records out—the neighborhood support was always there. Nowadays, you have to have a record out to maintain a tour and get current air play and so forth. Fortunately, we were able to work clubs and festivals around the world.

Our first international tour happened in 1982. Some guy from the Groningen Festival in Holland had contacted Kidd Jordan (he had been over there before), and he put us in touch with them. Shortly after that, George Wein of Festival Productions brought us over for our first real tour—we did Nice, Perugia, some stuff in Spain. That was in 1984. George brought us up to New York to do a couple of his festivals there. Some clubs in New York heard we were coming, and we got booked at a club called Tramp's for a week and the Village Gate for a couple of weeks. Man, it went so well that by the time we came back from Europe, they wanted us for two more weeks at the Village Gate and another week at Tramp's. My wife was pregnant at the time, and what started as a two-week tour extended to six weeks. I was ready to go home, but two days before we were due to fly back, George Wein called me and wanted me to meet some lawyers and booking agents. I told him, "I have to go home."

It was happening real fast. When I got home at the end of the six weeks, I was getting calls from promoters in California who wanted me to come out there the following week. That ended up being a four-week trip. That year, between July and December, we went to Europe four times. Europe made me aware that there were people outside New

Orleans—in fact outside the United States—that were listening to what we were doing. I found we were more widely accepted in Europe than in most of America. New Orleans was different; we began there, and we were very successful locally. Before we started traveling, we were doing two or more gigs a day, five or six days a week. We worked a lot.

Outside Louisiana, support was in pockets. It was OK in California, but our widest acceptance was in Europe. I had heard that, but you don't know how it is until you actually go there. There were many more festivals and clubs that featured jazz, and a high level of enthusiasm. We got the same sort of reception in Japan. We'd play clubs that held four hundred people, play three shows a night, empty the place each time, and fill it back up for each show, which was obviously good for the pocket.

I can still see the concert when we recorded the Mardi Gras at Montreux album. That was back in 1986, but I can still remember going out to play in that auditorium. It was so powerful, so electric! I can still feel it. A couple of years previously, when we were in Europe, we had experienced this thing where it doesn't get dark. We were sitting up, talking and drinking and playing around, waiting for it to get dark so we'd know what time to go to bed. Then it was six o'clock in the morning, and we saw people coming out to go to work.

It was the same kind of thing in Montreux. We had already been over there for about three weeks before we played the gig. We'd been up all night, and we thought, "Who in the world is going to come out and hear a band at two o'clock in the morning?" But when we walked out on the stage, the venue was packed. People were cheering and clapping from beginning to end. Freddie Hubbard and Curtis Fuller had already played, and so had Herbie Hancock and his band, and Howard Johnson.

So finally we went on, and as the night was going on, I was worried that it was getting late, and the venue would be empty. The place held several hundred people, but it sounded like thousands. The lights were on us, and I really couldn't see the people, but I remember the feeling of all that energy in the room. I had forgotten we were recording the concert. I still remember the guys and what we were doing on stage. When we walked off at the end, they brought us back for two encores. By then we were tired. It was probably around five o'clock in the morning, and we had to catch a flight at eight. It was a pretty special event.

When Kirk and Charles Joseph left the band, it was 1991. By then we were doing about two hundred dates a year, which is a lot. We'd get into a city at twelve o'clock in the afternoon, do a sound check, get some dinner, do the show. I like to leave right after the show, so we were traveling pretty much all the time. The traveling was beginning to wear on everyone. I don't know what made the Joseph brothers decide to leave, but I'm sure the traveling had a lot to do with it. When we had to replace them, we had a whole summer tour booked—about four months solid work. There was no time to think about their replacements. We were actually at the airport on the way to Canada when I found out that they weren't coming—they had decided not to do it anymore.

I got off the plane at Indianapolis, made some phone calls, and confirmed that they definitely weren't coming. So I had to make arrangements to audition some bass players in Canada. It was rough—I was already dead tired from a tour we had just finished on the West Coast. I had figured to get a day off in Canada and catch up on some sleep, but instead, I had to call ahead and arrange to audition electric bass players. And when we chose one, we had to rehearse fifteen songs to make it through the show. Then we had to play a couple of dates in Detroit. But when we got to the U.S. border, the border police wouldn't let us bring the Canadian bass player with us. So when we got to Detroit, I had to audition bass players again.

After that, we had three days back in New Orleans to find replacements on trombone and sousaphone, because we were leaving for a tour of Southeast Asia. That tour lasted until maybe a week before Christmas, and by then we had decided that we would take January off to be with our families. Then I was back on the road again.

One of the things I got from Danny Barker, and I learned playing around New Orleans, was that when people go out, they really want to be entertained. A lot of musicians thought that when you went out on a gig, you had to play like John Coltrane or Charlie Parker. It had to be real difficult for the audience to understand—and that's not true. People do come to a show that are really interested in the music, but most people just want to be entertained.

That's how I knew how to make the night work, both for the audience and for the band. If it's going well for the band, then the audience will be happy. Because we used the same group of people all the time, we knew when there were humorous musical things happening that maybe had started somewhere else but just carried on on the stage, and that made it fun and bearable to do those six- or seven-week trips.

The Jelly Roll project came about from a suggestion of our record producer, Scott Billington. The first record we did with Scott was Mardi Gras in Montreux. We had such a good rapport with him, when we changed record labels, he made the move with us. The new company suggested that we try something a little bit different, so we came up with the Morton idea. At that time I really didn't know too much about Jelly Roll Morton's music.

At the time we agreed to do it, we were getting ready to do another long European trip. So I said, "If we do this, y'all gonna help us with the music. I have none, no CDs, no written music, nothing." While we were on tour, I got deliveries of music at airports, train stations, hotels, all different places. I landed in Paris and heard them calling my name on the intercom. It was some music and CDs for the project. So we chose the songs while we were on the road, rehearsed as we traveled. I did some of the charts, Wardell Quezergue did some, Freddy Kemp did some, and Tom McDermott did one. I wrote mine mainly on airplanes.

When we got back, Wardell had had six weeks to work on the stuff like everybody else, but I think he forgot when we were coming home. The night I got back, we had a rehearsal scheduled for the next day. I called him and said, "Have you got the charts ready?" He said, "Oh, yeah, I got 'em." But I knew he really didn't.

We went ahead and rehearsed the music that Ed Frank had done and that Fred Kemp had done. We didn't hear from Wardell that day, but then the next day he called and said, "OK, I got your charts now." I later found out that he'd written them all in a day and a half. And Wardell doesn't play piano—he did the charts with a tuning fork! That's truly amazing.

The Jelly Roll project in itself was very, very interesting and gratifying and educational because it brought a dimension to the band that we didn't have. Even today, we still get requests to play tunes from that album. It was a good change of pace. When you're out on the road, you can fall into a rut of playing the same songs all the time, but we've been fortunate in that we've had other things to draw upon.

We were traveling a lot—we weren't doing a lot of street things, we were just doing festivals and college performances. So the need to keep it as a brass band wasn't there. It was all just music anyway, and I didn't care whether they called it a brass band or not.

The next big change was in 1994, when my drummers felt the need to make some changes. That was Lionel Batiste and Jenell Marshall. Jenell's wife had been getting ill on and off over the years, and Lionel had a son who was having marital difficulties. We thought we'd just find two more drummers, but it's not that easy. Those two had worked so closely together for all those years: you can replace the people, but you can't replace that closeness. I talked it over with the guys and said, "Look, we're not going to find two guys who are going to walk in here and do the same thing that Jenell and Lionel were doing. Why don't we just try one guy playing the whole kit?"

We were just going out on a rock and roll tour with a group called the Black Crowes. We knew every night there would be around six thousand people, and we wanted to make the best impression. So we hired a drummer and a keyboard player, and it worked. We did seventy-two shows in about ninety days. Then we thought, "OK, let's add a guitar player and see what happens." That's how the band goes out now.

When I first went up to New York in 1984, there was a woman called Marie St. Louis who worked with George Wein. She had said to me then, "One day you're going to get tired of this." They knew what I was in for, and I didn't.

Any time I was in New York, I'd have lunch or dinner with George and Marie. One day I woke up in New York, looked in the mirror, and thought, "I'm tired of this shit." I had thought the same thing many times before, but this time I was serious. I called George, and he told me, "When you get back to New Orleans, give Quint Davis a call." When I made the call, Quint took me out to lunch and we worked something out. This was in August 1998.

I talked it over with my wife and then went round to the guys' homes and spoke to them individually, starting with Roger. They didn't say much at the time, but I could tell that it rattled them a little bit. I didn't hear from them, so I called a meeting. They said, "If you feel you need to do this, go ahead and do it." At the same time, we had a theater tour booked and some stuff in China. I still had to participate in those things, but my ultimate goal was to get off the road and go back to school.

So in September 1998, I came to work at Festival Productions to book the acts for Storyville. Then after that I agreed to start doing the booking for Jazz Fest. That led to other stuff, and now I do private bookings, and I do work for other festivals. That's how I saw my way out of having to travel all the time. I still want to play, and I still want to make some trips.

I remember the first night I wasn't with the band; I don't think I had ever missed a gig. The night they were leaving town without me, I was unsettled. My wife noticed it. I was laying in bed that night—there was a clock by the bed, one on the TV, another one on a shelf. I was thinking "OK, it's eight o'clock, they're leaving. Twelve o'clock, they're on stage." I had to jump in the car and take a ride. But I knew I would be working with them in November and again in January.

So it was like a gradual weaning for me. It took the better part of a year to realize that I didn't have to travel anymore. It felt good. I had the chance to spend that year with the family. Working for Festival Productions, I was just as busy, I was working round the clock. But the big difference is I was home.

Roger Lewis, Saxophones

BORN: New Orleans, October 5, 1941

Long-term member of Fats Domino's band before joining the Dirty Dozen Brass Band, which he has been with for twenty-five years

Interviewed at his home on Myrtle Street, October 2002

Roger Lewis, Jackson Square, 1986

Photo by Marcel Joly

When I came to music was round the age of eight, or even younger than that, because that's when I started to take piano lessons. I was raised on Pleasant and Harmony Streets: Pleasant on one side, and Harmony on the other! As I remember, when I was a kid, I had a fascination with the saxophone—I would roll up a newspaper and make like I was playing. I can remember this stuff just like it was yesterday—I can see it, you don't forget stuff like that.

I heard the sound of the saxophone—the first sax that my dad bought was a tenor—that's when I was about ten years old. There was a record out called "Feel So Good" by Shirley and Lee. Everybody was trying to learn Lee Allen's saxophone solo off that. I was in junior high school.

In those days you could come out of junior high school with a trade—woodwork, sheet metal, auto mechanics, homemaking—everything that you need to survive, all from the public school system. 'Cause everybody's not going to college, you know? It's not like that now—they pulled all those programs. It's a whole nother thing now. And they had music programs, and the schools had bands—all the schools used to compete; they had contests and all that. The thing was, I wanted to play music in the joints, where it was happening, you know?

The first thing I did when I got my saxophone was I took it loose. Took everything off it, stripped it down.

My first live performance was with a guy named Sylvester. He was a drummer, he used to come over by the house. What this cat did, he used to have a couple of twigs and

77

play a garbage can on the rim. We thought we was playing—we were just kids having fun.

So anyway, we moved downtown, and we hooked up a little band with some guys around the neighborhood. The Lastie brothers lived in the next block. They had a guy called Ornette Coleman—he was staying with the Lastie brothers. I used to hear those guys—he lived in the upstairs house, and I would be in the kitchen. I never had the courage to go over there—I probably would have learned a whole lot of stuff if I had knocked on that door at that time.

Anyway, we hooked up a little band round the neighborhood; we were playing at the Café Theater. We were young kids—we had plenty of energy. We had no car; we used to have to physically carry the drums and all that stuff. We're talking about a whole mile, man.

Then I got hooked up with another guy—he was a tenor player—and the first paid gig we did was at a little placed called Mabel's Tavern, on Magazine. They'd sit down and listen to us. I had to "walk the bar": the guy told us, "I want you to walk the bar, knock all the drinks over, so the drunks can buy some more alcohol."

You'd run out the front door, come in through the back door, slide on the floor honking your horn. Four-piece band—guitar, drums, bass, and me. I learned showmanship. I made so much money playing that horn. We went home with forty-seven dollars in change apiece. And when you did a back flip! People had never seen nothing like that. In those days, people was earning a hundred dollars a week—if you had a dollar, you was rich. So that was my first paying gig.

Then I hooked up with the Impressions—Curtis Mayfield was the guitar player in that band. We could listen to a song and play it just like the record. And John Moore, he would sound like the cat who was singing the song on the record. Our instrumentation was alto, tenor, and baritone saxes—I played tenor. On tenor, you can do all kinds of stuff—you can sound like a trumpet player, alto, whatever. When we played big gigs, we would have Eddie King on trombone, and we would maybe hire an extra drummer. Al Miller was our regular drummer. Earl Derbigny was the bass player, Henry Joseph was the baritone player, Sam Bijou was on piano. And we would have Alvin Alcorn and his son on trumpets to fill out the horn section.

This band never had no charts—we never had a written piece of music. Everybody had good ears. Bobby Blue Bland had a song called "Cry, Cry, Cry." We did a show with him. We would learn a song as soon as it came out. With us being kids, we was the opening band—we would play all his songs before he came on. When you're kids, you do stuff like that. And he wanted to know, where did we get the arrangements. Like, we had just listened to the records—it wasn't no big thing. As a matter of fact, when we played at the Dew Drop, he came over and sat in with us. There was no pain—you do that sort of thing now, people would get pissed off, but back then, it was a whole different thing.

So after that band, I was playing rhythm 'n' blues, rock 'n' roll, you know? All the artists that came through had to have a backup band, if they didn't have a band.

In 1971, I joined Fats Domino's band. Herbert Hardesty was in the band. Clarence
Brown was playing drums, and Fred Kemp. Then later on Lee Allen came back in the
band, and Dave Bartholomew. When I first went in the band . . . see, I got in after a guy
called Nat Perilliat died. They had Henry Joseph, the baritone player from the Impressions, and I made the transition. See, I was a tenor player. My baritone playing really
had started when I was playing with Eddie Bo [Edwin Bocage]—check "Mr. Popeye"
and all them songs. The band broke up, but I stayed on tenor. Then I got Fred Kemp in
that band, also on tenor.

I brought a baritone to rehearsal one day, and he said, "Hey man, you sound good on that
baritone." I wound up playing baritone. That's what happened—it started with Eddie Bo.

Anyhow, back to Fats Domino: Dave Bartholomew came back to the band—I think
him and Fats was feudin' or something. We had Herbert Hardesty, Walter Kimball,
Freddie Kemp, and me on saxes. People say that was the best band Fats ever had—we
were all around the same age, and we used to practice all the time together. And after
that band, we had Dave Bartholomew, Lee Allen, Walter Kimball, Smokey Johnson,
Jimmy Moyet, Walter Lastie. At one time, we would have three drummers set up on the
stage at the same time. It was crazy—at one time, we had two baritone players. The other
baritone player didn't really play—he was kind of an alcoholic—I'd be up there blowing
my ass off, man. He was a good saxophone player—he could really cut it—but he was
drunk half the time.

Then I joined Irma Thomas, who was playing down the road; I went to hear her, and
she said, "Where's your horn?" I said, "At home, in the cupboard." She said, "Go get it."
She paid me for the gig. It was around that time that Fats decided to take a long vacation.

I knew a guy called Daryl Adams, an alto player. Daryl said, "How you going to eat?
Start playing second line parades!" I was like, "Why not?" I made this gig with those
cats—I met Charles Joseph and started doing a lot of those parade gigs. That was the first
street work I had done. My early experience was with big bands.

I used to go to William Houston for music lessons—he had this music school. Charles
Joseph and Daryl Adams and those cats, they was already doing that Dirty Dozen thing.
It wasn't called the Dirty Dozen—that really started when I got in it. All of the Dirty
Dozen, they all have a different story to tell, different from my story. We hooked up—it
wasn't really organized to the level of where it is today. We started rehearsing.

Before the band started taking that shape, we started with Benny Jones. Benny's a
real sociable guy; he had all the parade gigs. Benny used to play with Lionel Batiste, kind

of entertainment for the neighborhood. What happened, he used to hire musicians, like Charles Joseph, Cyrille Salvant, Big Daddy [Andrew Green]. Big Daddy and Benny were the perfect drum combination.

Cyrille, the trumpet player, would not improvise. In New Orleans music, when you're going down the street, somebody got to be playing that melody. This cat Cyrille, he was great for that—he'd play the melody all day. You play a four-hour parade, he's going to be playing the melody—put all the colors you want around it, but he'd play the melody. You going to hear the song all the time.

That particular band in the beginning was Benny, Big Daddy, sometimes Kirk Joseph, sometimes Tuba Fats, but he was with the Olympia at that time. Gregory Davis came in, then Efrem Towns. Benny was working for the electric company, so he couldn't take a lot of gigs out of town. Lionel Batiste's son came in on drum.

We played our own music—what happened, we used to play a lot of traditional songs like "South Rampart Street Parade," "Didn't He Ramble," all the other songs that most bands wasn't even playing really. Then we started bringing in other stuff—I introduced "Night Train" to the band. People would play "Night Train" in bar rooms—it was like a stripper routine. We brought it to the streets. The first time we played it out there, the older musicians said, "Oh no, y'all can't play that! That kind of music don't go—you can't do that on the street!" The people loved it!

We played music slightly faster, and hyped up. We started playing original things, too. We had a parade uptown, around Magazine Street; it was about six o'clock in the morning. We started playing "Reveille"—we put all other things with it, and it just became a song. It came together on the street—"The Flintstones Meet the President" and "Blue Monk"—no brass band in the city played that before, we started that.

We would be going down the street swinging; there was a lot of creativity within the group. What made the difference was the beat was slightly faster. So, like, if you got heavy tennis shoes on, or jiving shoes on, we used to roll. Like, before, it was kind of in between; when we came along, we moved it faster. You had to be in good physical condition—we had guys dancing to us that was doing incredible things with their bodies. So the combination of picking up the beat, incorporating all things like Duke Ellington's "Caravan" and Charlie Parker's "Bongo Beep" and "Dexterity"—that's what made everything different.

We weren't thinking consciously about changing the music, but being in a band where you could do whatever you want to do, whatever musical ideas you had that you couldn't do with nobody else—bring it to the table, let's try it. I may not like it, but we'll do it—you have an idea you want to blow, go on and blow! The music has its structure, and we do have written music now, like the Jelly Roll Morton album. We hired people to write that; it was orchestrated.

Dirty Dozen Brass Band
Courtesy Dave Cirilli, Big Hassle

We did a rap thing, a CD called Ears to the Wall—*I was trying to get copies of it to sell on gigs. The record company can't find it—we did it, but it don't exist. You can buy everything else, but you can't buy that one. I think that's what made the difference with the group, because everybody had freedom to do what they wanted musically—you didn't have one guy saying, "I don't want to hear that. This is the way it has to go—you play my music, later for what you do."*

Over the years, we've recorded with a lot of different people, too. We've recorded with Dizzy Gillespie, Elvis Costello, Danny Barker, Dr. John. Dizzy was crazy about the band. We used to play at a club called the Glasshouse, uptown. Anything might happen there. Little small place, a bit bigger than these two rooms [around 12 by 25 feet]. Put fifty people in there, you had a crowd. Sometimes, we'd have a hundred and fifty. So anyway, every Monday they'd have free red beans and rice, and they'd charge a dollar to come in. So there's Dizzy Gillespie sitting there at the table. When we came out the back room, we'd be ready, you know what I'm saying? Everybody would come through that place.

Being a saxophone player and hanging out with Freddie Kemp—this cat was a genius on that saxophone, man. If you wanted to keep up with cats like that, you'd study Charlie Parker. When we was on the road together, Kemp would say, "Play your major scales." Now, I had learned at high school . . . they teach you to read music, and that's it. Kemp would say, "Play all twelve of them." I'm like, "They got twelve of them?" He said, "Look, man. Before you even start talking about music, you gotta know scales. I'm going to give you a week to learn your major scales." Then he moved on to the tri-

ads—that man was like a conservatory, man. He would call you at three o'clock in the morning and play stuff on the saxophone—you had to shed it. He would write two bars, and you couldn't play it—that's how bad he was. Incredible technique. One of his favorites was Johnny Griffin, and he was the fastest saxophone player in the world. Anyway, the band developed, and we ended up playing Carnegie Hall.

Then we began touring in Europe. The audiences were great—I mean the reception was fabulous. We played a concert with the Buddy Rich Band. I remember playing opposite Count Basie. We played four weeks at the Village Gate—no band had done that before. It wasn't no sudden thing—before all that, we were playing baseball games, house parties, street gigs—the band really got popular from all those second line parades.

It's really stressful being on the road all the time. I call what we got now the new band; see, what's happening right now, we're jamming. The scene keeps changing—right now, we're the world's greatest jam band. We still function as a brass band—we did a concert recently where we marched through the crowd, thousands of people. A lot of kids haven't been exposed to this kind of stuff. Now, personally speaking, I loved the band with me, Gregory, Efrem, Charles and Kirk, Kevin Harris, and Lionel. If that band was together now, seriously, there ain't no telling musically speaking, what heights we would have reached.

Not taking anything away from our guitar player—I mean, I came up playing with guitar players. I always wanted to play with just horns and drums—for some reason, you got more freedom, and horns can do just about anything. I mean, we've had Richard Knox, and Carl Leblanc (he's a personal friend of mine) on organ, so we've had a full rhythm section with us. But you take all that stuff out, just leave the horns—O Lord! You can make a chord be whatever you want it to be.

We get guitar players and piano players with us, and they can't see where they can fit. Richard Knox, he figured it out, then he quit! I said to him, "O Lord, not now!"

I liked the band the way it was. The band we got now is a great band, and we have some of the finest musicians on the planet Earth—Sammy Williams ain't no joke! He's the loudest trombone player in the world, and he has unbelievable energy and showmanship—he's about 260 pounds, about six foot three, size eighteen shoes—he ain't no more than about twenty years old. He'll dance all night—I don't know how he does it. I'm soloing, and I'm thinking people are clapping for me—they're clapping for him and his dancing; they don't pay me any attention.

One thing I find very flattering is we go to a lot of colleges and universities—and the bands there have transcribed a lot of our things—so there's three other baritones sounding like me playing my part note for note. They've written all the stuff out—some of it wasn't written in the first place!

Benny Jones, Drums

Founding member of the Dirty Dozen Brass Band; founder and leader of the Tremé Brass Band

Interviewed on South Park Place, September 2001

Elliott Callier, Benny Jones
Photo by Marcel Joly

I was born here in New Orleans, at 1024 North Robertson Street. I came from a very large family—seven brothers and six sisters. My daddy was a drummer, Chester Jones. The only other one of our family that played music was my half brother, Eugene Jones; he used to play with Clarence "Frogman" Henry on Bourbon Street. I had a younger brother called Michael George—he used to play bass drum in the band. Eugene died in the late sixties.

My father had also been a prizefighter in his younger days. Lots of people have told me how good he was—I never got to see him fight. I remember when I was young and we lived on Marais Street—the old Caldonia was in that neighborhood. And Mama Ruth had the Cozy Corner on Robertson. And there were lots of jazz funerals in the neighborhood, two or three times a week. So my daddy was playing around a lot—sometimes I'd see him with Louis Cottrell, and sometimes with Placide Adams.

Sometimes at the weekend, he'd be doing a jazz funeral together with Freddie Kohlman. Freddie would say, "Chuck, what do you want to play?" If my daddy chose snare drum, Freddie would play bass drum. Or the other way around—it didn't matter to them.

Kid Howard lived on Marais Street, and so did Jim Robinson until he moved over onto St. Philip.

I was born and raised in the Tremé area, and I've never left it. Half the musicians in New Orleans came out of the Tremé—my father, Smokey Johnson, John Boudreaux, the list goes on and on.

I got interested in second lining behind all those old men when they played the jazz funerals. The Sixth Ward Diamonds, the Sixth Ward High Steppers, the Money Wasters, I

was in all those clubs. We would get about twenty of us and then vote on what colors we would wear, what color shoes. We used to buy the matching cloth at the store and have it made up into outfits.

What they would do is, they would put up a sign in a bar saying there was a social and pleasure club starting. We're going to meet on, let's say, the third Sunday of every month. Everybody would come, but if we started getting too many members, say more than twenty-five or thirty, we'd shut the book down, and tell people membership was closed. Members would pay a joining fee, usually about forty or fifty dollars. At the end of the year, they'd split up any money that was left and start again the next year.

The main reason for the clubs was parading. It's not like a benevolent society, which has to have a charter from the city and would be responsible for paying deceased members' burial expenses, or a band for the funeral, or whatever. This would be less formal, and most of the money went to buy the clothes. Some clubs would only parade two or three times a year and some of them only once. My daddy used to belong to the Square Deal Social and Pleasure Club; I think he was on the baseball team.

I was always following musicians when I was younger—I married into the Batiste family, they were always having parties—I used to be beating on the pots and pans, and that's how I got started. I taught myself, no outside teaching.

My daddy was pleased when I started to play. Sometimes when he worked with Placide Adams, they might have to march from the Royal Sonesta Hotel to the boat. Placide would ask me to play snare drum for the march while my daddy was sitting up on the boat for the sit-down gig. I joined the union in 1976.

I was around sixteen when I started. Like I say, we always had parties, and the Batiste family had a kazoo band, with the Baby Dolls and all that. I bought a bass drum and started banging round the house with it, trying to learn that beat, you know? As a matter of fact, I started off doing a couple of gigs with the Olympia Brass Band as grand marshal.

The bandleader was in charge of the actual jobs, because he had to get the money to pay everybody. He'd tell the grand marshal, "OK, we're going to make a short route. Go down four blocks and take a left," etc.

When we started on the street, we brought people into the Tremé on Halloween or St. Joseph's night. The Tremé Brass Band plays more the traditional music—blues and hymns and gospel tunes—and the Rebirth plays like modern music, funk and so forth. We can play that too, but we stick more to the traditional music—so far, we've made more money with the traditional music, so I just stay right there. My father being a musician really helped me, because I got to meet a bunch of his friends, and that helped me get started later on.

Tremé Brass Band (Kenneth Terry, Kerwin James, Lionel Batiste Sr., Revert Andrews; kneeling: Butch Gomez, Benny Jones) *Courtesy Butch Gomez*

The way the young bands dress and play for a funeral today, I never thought I'd see it happening. Now they come in short pants, cap, you know? Sometimes those young bands ask me to play with them. I guess they respect me because of my connection with the Dirty Dozen and the way that band changed music. But after I left the Dirty Dozen, I went back to the traditional stuff.

The first band to change the music was years ago, Leroy Jones and the Hurricane Brass Band. And the next one after that was the Dirty Dozen. It was modern times, modern music, the new steps in the modern way of dancing: it all changed the tempo of music. The audience had a lot to do with how the music changed. The young people today, if they want up-tempo music, they'll hire a younger band. If people want a traditional funeral, they'll hire us to play the old dirges, dress in the traditional way.

When I was young, I would see the Onward, the Eureka, the Olympia, the Tuxedo, all those old bands. They were more traditional than my band—they had clarinets, for instance, I don't.

I started on bass drum with Harold Dejan's second band, Olympia No. 2. One time Andrew Jefferson got sick, and they took me to Mexico with the first band. Andrew showed me a few things on the gigs, like, "Hum the tune to yourself—that way you don't get lost."

* * *

When me and my wife was young ones, courting, I was playing with the Dirty Dozen kazoo band. I told you, my wife was a member of the Batiste family, and the kazoo band used to walk behind the Baby Dolls at Mardi Gras. All the Batiste ladies, Felicia, Mary, all them, were in the Baby Dolls. In the kazoo band was Lionel's brothers—Henry, Norman, "Precisely," Arthur. It was all the Batiste family; they lived on St. Philip Street, right across from the Nelson family. They always had parties going on, with kazoos, singing, drumming, ukulele, all that. They'd play old songs like "Margie"—that was what they called the Dirty Dozen.

Then I set about forming the Dirty Dozen Brass Band. Originally, there was me, Andrew Green on snare drum, Kirk Joseph, Roger Lewis, Charles Joseph, Cyrille Salvant (who used to play with the Majestic). I was the leader; I put the band together. Sometimes, people asked me to supply two bands on the same day—it wasn't a problem. I'd use people like Tuba Fats or Richard Payne to make up the other band.

It was the Dirty Dozen name that got us started, and then our music changed everything around. A friend of mine called me to play Monday nights at the Glasshouse on Saratoga Street. We'd start around ten thirty and play until two or three in the morning—I think the admission was three dollars. We'd make up tunes on the spot. Roger Lewis was technically the best in the band, and Kirk Joseph had plenty of energy. We had Kevin Harris on tenor saxophone, Charles Joseph on trombone.

Some of the band had worked for the Olympia, some of them came from the Majestic Brass Band, some from the Tuxedo, some of them from the Hurricane. The band thought if they started changing their music, it would bring them onto a different level.

We got a recording date with George Wein—we had a five-year recording contract with him. As the band got more famous, it started picking up plenty of work and going in and out of town.

I had a good job, my kids were in high school, and I couldn't always leave town to be with the band. I worked with them for a while when they had work in New Orleans, but then I decided to branch out with the Tremé Brass Band and play the traditional stuff, because not too many other people were doing that. Roger Lewis and Gregory Davis started running the Dirty Dozen after I left.

I started the Tremé band with me, Lionel Batiste, James Andrews on trumpet, Corey Henry on trombone, sometimes Keith Anderson on trombone too. For a while, Butch Gomez played soprano, and he did some booking too. We did real well by coming back to the traditional music.

"Uncle" Lionel Paul Batiste Sr., Bass Drum

BORN: New Orleans, November 2, 1932

Member of the Tremé Brass Band

Interviewed on South Park Place, September 2001

Troy "Trombone Shorty" Andrews,
Lionel Batiste Sr.

Photo by Peter Nissen

I was born and raised in the Tremé. I'm not related to any other musicians with the same name. My daddy was Walter Lewis Batiste—he was from outside of New Orleans. He moved here when he was young, and that's when he met my momma. He was a blacksmith; he used to shoe horses. Then he quit that job after he was pushed by one of the mules. My momma's name was Alma Trepagnier Batiste. I have four sisters and six brothers.

I was the youngest of the eleven—all my brothers played guitar and banjo. In the area where I was raised up was right across from Craig School. Around the corner at 933 Marais Street, Jim Robinson lived, the trombone player. In the thirteen hundred block was Little Jim, Sidney Brown—he played upright bass and tuba. And in the fifteen hundred block, that's where Kid Howard was living. On St. Claude, that's where Alton Purnell the piano player lived. I knew all of those fellows. In the twelve hundred block of St. Philip Street, that's where Arthur Ogle the snare drummer lived. The nine hundred block of St. Claude Street was where Willie Parker was. And "Bazooka Noone" [Johnson] was in the neighborhood. And Smiley Lewis, Cousin Joe—I was around all them. They saw I was interested. I always liked to be around musicians. At one time, I was playing a little piccolo.

Where we were living at was across from the school. And when the school band would be rehearsing, I would be on the step, playing drums along with them. My daddy bought a drum for me. There was an upright bass player, name of Halsey, walked with a limp. And Slow Drag and Mr. Alphonse Picou. George Lewis is related to me. My daddy showed George Lewis, so I understand, how to play a nickel flute. My daddy played guitar and banjo too. He mostly entertained us, people in the neighborhood.

I knew Burnell Santiago when he lived on St. Claude Street; we all came up around that area. He was living right behind St. Philip. He was good—you couldn't fool with him. He played all kinds, including classical. My daddy had all kinds of instruments in the house, except a horn. I used to fool with all of them, even the piano. My sister was going to lessons. I'd be alongside, and I'd watch them. My oldest brother played piano too—in those days, everybody's house you went to, they had a piano. I learned how to play "Salty Dog."

My mom used to sing a lot, and my oldest sister. All of us could entertain. Like we'd gather round the piano, have some wine, have a party. Right in the Tremé—I'm very proud of the Tremé. I used to take a piece of wood, tap dance to the music—I must have been around nine years old. My first job was for Benny Jones's daddy, Mr. Chester. Benny had an uncle played piano. The job was across the river, a place called the Pepper Pot. Professor Longhair, Smiley Lewis, a lot of them played over there.

And right there on St. Philip and Burgundy was a barroom called the Honey Dripper. That's where Smiley Lewis, Cousin Joe, and Walter Nelson played. Walter was living across the street, in a rooming house called the Monkey Puzzle. His son, Walter Junior—they called him Papoose—he got his break with Fats Domino. Papoose was a better player than his daddy, except for the blues—you can't beat those old men for playing blues. He had a little brother—they called him Prince La La—he had in mind that he could play better than Papoose, but he couldn't. And he had an aunt called Black Emma—she played the hell out of the banjo. Her right name was Emma Guichard. People would come from outside the Tremé to play. Like the dance nights on the weekend. They all used to go in the yard at the Monkey Puzzle and practice.

I haven't played guitar or banjo for a long while, but I still have an instrument. I mostly chord, but as soon as I get into a groove, a string pops. I sang in the church choir. My ma and my uncle used to sing all the time. They'd spin the bottle. If it stopped on you, you had to sing. Another thing they'd do, you had to dance with the bottle. You put the wine bottle on the floor, and you take your two feet, and you move like that. And you sing, "Joli palme, joli palme on beau ai, joli palme on beau, que bec se, joli palme on beau, joli palme. . . ." Move round the bottle and cut back up. After you did that, if the bottle lay flat, you had to buy some wine. You used a fifth bottle. You could take that down to the barroom, put a funnel in it, fill it right up. A pint of wine like that would cost you about thirty-five cents. At the bar, you could get a ten-cent shot or a fifteen-cent shot. Muscatel and like that.

In the Tremé, the majority were beer and wine drinkers. They didn't care too much about whiskey. When I was a young boy, I used to hate that. I used to wash all them bottles to make the home brew. That would be hard liquor too. Them old people would cap the bottles. You'd be laying in your bed at night and all of a sudden, "Boom! Boom!" The bottles would explode.

The police would walk the beat in the Tremé. They were all white. They mostly got on OK with the people, but maybe two or three of them didn't. They were, you know, a little more stiffer than the others. They would walk the beat, and when they got to the corner, they would hit that nightstick, and that let you know that they were around. But some of them got along without a stick. Just doing their job. When we played dice on the corner, we used to have to run from them. They'd creep up on you at the corner to make you run. Then they'd pick up the money and split. Playing dice was legal, but not on the sidewalk. Sometimes they'd throw the nightstick at you.

I remember once on Barracks and St. Claude, someone took the nightstick and hand-cuffed the damn policeman. He heard no more about that. But the policeman lost his job. It was like, "If you can whip my butt you can go free, but if I win, you're going to have a butt whipped and you're going to jail."

I was mischievous—I wasn't bad. Some of those boys I came up with were real bad boys. They'd drop out of school, start doing the wrong things. They'd wind up at what they called doing their "college"—they'd be locked up in jail. They didn't do like it is now, you know, shooting. They would fight—I've seen a fellow bust me in the head with a Jax beer bottle—it hurt, too. Go by the drugstore, get them to shave around the cut, put a little iodine or Mercurochrome on it, put a patch. Then I went right back to the barroom—the one that busted my head was in there. But it was over with. His eye was puffed up, I had a patch on my head, but it was over with. But now, someone just can't stand to be a loser.

The square right on Galvez near Banks, they called that Nanny Goat Square. There was a whole lot of fights that they would meet at Nanny Goat Square. They would say, "I'll meet you in the square," and they would give them a time. Cabbage Alley was around Perdido Street. They had a lot of musicians down there—it was almost like a [red light] district—fast women. Near the battlefield. They had a whole lot of pimps, too, in there.

When I was young I liked to go dancing to Sidney Desvigne and Herb Leary. I remember he had a big old bus—on the back it was light blue and dark blue. We'd go to a dance and do the Trucking, the Suzie Q, and when it came to waltzing—you can't touch me for waltzing. But these days, you can't get a youngster . . . if you gave them a thousand dollars, they can't waltz. Me, Papoose, a fellow by the name of Chin, we all used to go to the dances. I used to like the kind of music that Sidney Desvigne played, real sentimental. He'd play the hell out of that song called "In the Mood." And then, after he started getting away, he went to the coast—that's when Dave Bartholomew came in. At the Famous Door after World War II, that's where Sharkey Bonano used to perform.

I used to dance in the street, for nickels and dimes—me and this fellow called Bird, we'd be dancing on Bourbon Street. When we got to St. Philip, where we would turn to come back to the Tremé, we would sit on a step and count the money.

We would go to dances at the San Jacinto Club. The Autocrat Club, it was a question of complexion—they'd hold a paper bag up, and if you was darker than the bag, they wouldn't let you in. The guy that ran it, he was kind of passe à blanc. *And Edwin "Beansie" Fauria had something to do with it. There was a girl in the neighborhood— name was Doris, pretty girl, spoke real well—she took me there. She told them, "If you don't let him in here I'm going to call my father. My daddy is a big-time judge. I'll get him to come down here." Her father was nothing but a riverfront worker!*

They were all mixed people in the Tremé. Ursuline Street, from the river to Bayou St. John, there was white both sides. From the French Quarter, St. Philip had black and white next door to one another. And all them houses from Rampart had slave quarters to the back, generally two rooms, with an outhouse in between. They got along with no trouble.

We didn't have a segregation problem in the Tremé area. We would sit down together in the house and eat. You didn't have all that robbing in those days. In that neighborhood, they had real feelings for one another; they loved one another. So there wasn't no hard times. The white would look out for the black, the black would raise the white kids. I've seen a sister nurse a black child on that side and a white child on this.

The barrooms had a wagon to go and get ice. It came from the icehouse on St. Peter between Claiborne and Robertson. On Marais and Dumaine, they had a sawmill there; the name was Lafitte. On St. Peter Street there was a lumberyard. My brother Norman, he had a goat. It would pull this little wagon round to pick up ice or to get charcoal for the furnace. One day he went over by my grandmother, and when he came back, he looked for the goat. But someone had ate it! Norman did some crying.

The Baby Dolls were my momma, my aunt, and the older women in the Tremé area. They came out masked at Carnival. They had the Baby Dolls, they had the Dirty Dozen, they had the Million Dollar Dolls. The night before Carnival, they would be drinking, playing the guitar, costuming for the Dirty Dozen. They got their name from the way they would mask. Some would take mustard and put it on the back of their leg, put a diaper on. Baby Dolls would wear a nice hat, short dresses. They'd wear the leg stockings, put paper money in there. But if you reached for the woman's leg, then you're in trouble. People lined up to see us come by; the Baby Dolls would dance and play tambourines.

When we started out, we played kazoos—that was what we had. I played the banjo. My oldest sister carried the bass line; she would bass into a gallon jug. You had the lead, you had harmonies—I would blow real high. I had a brother called Aitken—he could play so many riffs. That was the original Dirty Dozen Kazoo Band. We played at the Jazz Fest, with Alan Jaffe on bass horn. Got a big crowd round us.

When I was in school, I was on snare drum. And the fellow that played the bass drum, he was absent—he was ill. It was a real big old antique bass drum. I thought, "I can't tote that big old drum." I let that drum roll from upstairs downstairs, trying to break it.

I made my first set of drums: I made the foot pedal with an inner tube for a spring. The bass drum was a washtub, I beat it to tune it. And I used a slop bucket. The first band I played with was the Olympia. The first band I played out of town with was the Crescent City, with Dalton Rousseau, the trumpet player. The grand marshal was Anderson Minor.

I worked with Tuba Fats—to me, he's one of the finest tuba players you got. I'm the one that got him into the Olympia Band. Harold Dejan's related to my oldest sister-in-law.

When I was younger, I would go over by the Palace Theater—it was what they called vaudeville. Harold Dejan was performing there. I had a sister-in-law, she used to sing over there. Harold played saxophone on the vaudeville night. Anyone, black and white, could go to the Palace Theater—you could sit anywhere. It was on Dauphine, one block before Canal. It cost eighteen cents to get in. We used to go by the Gypsy Tea Room too.

Benny Jones is the one that put the Dirty Dozen Brass Band together. He couldn't travel like they wanted, because of his family. So he put my son to play drums with them. Then he started the Tremé Brass Band, which is a good band. See, the way Benny and I play with the Tremé band, we listen to the crowd—we have something to give the older ones: give them a chance to get up and dance, remember the time they first heard that number. If you're playing and nobody's interested, that's depressing to me. What the hell to play to make them get up? They sitting like they're in church.

Nowadays, the tempos are faster, and I find the young bands of today play school music. I could play with those young bands; I've played with the Rebirth. I have to play my music. The youngsters get their music from school and reading the music. The band teacher gets a hold of a tune that he would like, so he sits there and writes it, and they move it to a tempo where they can march with it. Sometimes it's not clear; in other words, it's not snappy. They play this number called "Casanova"—that's not a traditional song. You can't play that traditional—it should be mostly vocal. Everything is choppy. But the youngsters like it, and the dancing is different.

Tremé Brass Band at Freddie Kohlman's funeral, 1990 (Frederick Shepherd, Revert Andrews, Butch Gomez, Lionel Batiste Snr., Kerwin James) *Photo by Bill Dickens*

Of all the bands going today, the Tremé plays the most traditional. I've played with the Algiers band, and they play traditional too. When I was coming up, my favorite bass drum player was Emile Knox. And you had Willie Parker, I remember him. There was Earl Palmer—he was good—and John Boudreaux.

Michael White, he tries to keep that old-time thing going. I had a gig with him. So he tells me the dress code, and I say "I know, it's black and white." Well, we met up at Tulane, sitting round waiting. So I took the cap off. Michael says to me, "Uncle, your cap." I say, "Yeah, give me the hat band to put on it." He said, "No—will you take your pins off the hat?" Man, I have some pins on that hat—I had to take them all off. I haven't had time to put them all back on yet.

I miss New Orleans when I'm away. I remember once—we were overseas for Carnival. Everybody sitting around saying, "Man, I wonder what this one is doing. I wonder what's happening." One of the guys called home—the phone just rang, nobody answered. We said, "Man, your wife ain't home, she's out there somewhere." And it got to him.

When I go on the street now, I'm looking for a combination of things: the music, the money, and the girls. When you get up in age, everything slows up. I may not be able to do that long walking like I used to. So far, my legs are fine.

A Note on the Baby Dolls

The masking traditions carried on by Lionel Batiste's family go back in history almost as far as jazz itself. Beatrice Hill, who claimed to be "the first Baby Doll," recalled: "Liberty and Perdido was red hot back in 1912 when that idea started. And we decided to call ourselves the Million Dollar Baby Dolls. . . . I remember one nigger trying to tear my stockings open to get at my money till my man hit him over the head with a chair."[24]

Austin Leslie, interviewed for the Tremé Oral History Project, agreed the Baby Dolls were not to be messed with: "Then they had the Baby Dolls: all those women dressed like little babies, in hot pink and sky blue. You fool with them, they'd cut you too."[25]

It was indeed a colorful scene, as George Guesnon described it in a 1959 interview: "Gilbert Young took me to the Humming Bird Cabaret on Bienville and Marais on St. Joseph's night 1927, and what I saw there I ain't never saw before. It was the Baby Dolls. All those whores with their asses out, kicking high their pretty legs in the fancy lace stockings, filled with fifty and one hundred dollar bills. All them bitches were just having themselves a ball, you know?"[26]

These were no ordinary goings-on. "If a girl's dress wasn't way below the knee, people would knock her head off," explained Henry "Booker T" Glass. "The members of the Baby Dolls Club wore short dresses on Carnival Parades, but they also wore masks."[27]

As Earl Palmer (born 1924) recollected, "The Baby Dolls were women that masqueraded as little baby girls. It just started as a comedic gesture, these great big fat women in baby doll outfits, bonnets tied under their chins, and little socks, and sometimes they wore a diaper. Thighs this big sticking out of their tiny bloomers. Some of them got a little nasty sometimes. But we're talking about the days when they wasn't allowed to do anything real nasty, as opposed to now, when they show their pussies on Bourbon Street. The Baby Dolls wouldn't dare do that."[28]

Mac Rebennack (Dr. John) also recalls the Baby Dolls when he was growing up in the late 1940s and early 1950s, and the tradition seems to have evolved:

> One of the gangs was made up of all the whores and pimps from Perdido Street; their parade was called Gangster Molls and Baby Dolls. Everyone in

this group dressed as outlandishly as possible. The women wore eye-popping dresses; the ones who looked highest priced wore ultra-sharp women's suits, but with see-through bras underneath. Others wore slit miniskirts showing lace panties, stiletto heels, and flowing low-cut blouses. . . .

They were ridiculous and funny all at the same time. They'd come busting out of their dives during Mardi Gras, their dresses and suits lined with satin and glitter, real sharp-looking and hilarious. They'd march down the greens, that broad strip of grass that separates one side of the street from the other, cutting up, shakin' the bacon and carrying on, and everyone would back off to let them start high-steppin.' And you had best back off, too, because they took their kicks seriously.[29]

Jerry Brock believes he saw the last parade of the Baby Dolls:

I remember 1981, when I went out with the Kazoo Band and Baby Dolls. That was the last year they paraded. They invited me along. We met at Felicia's house. She was one of the Baby Dolls—she lived on Orleans Street. We had a big breakfast—eggs, pork chops, gumbo, biscuits. There were about twenty-five to thirty of us.

Everybody was prepared—making sure their costumes were right, making sure their instruments were as out of tune as possible. Then everybody got on their knees and said a prayer that God would keep them safe on Mardi Gras Day.

Then we hit the door. It was one of the most surreal things I've ever witnessed. It was like a Fellini experience. We sang all those bawdy songs, with a crowd of fifty or so joining in. Songs like "The Pecker Song," about a man that played with his pecker so much that his pecker wouldn't peck no more. I was just flabbergasted. We'd turn a corner, pull up in front of somebody's house, and there'd be a barren card table with a single bottle of whiskey on it. Everybody knew that it was for them, and a friend was honoring them on Mardi Gras. There might be a few finger sandwiches too.

So they'd hang around for a little bit, play a song or two, and then on to the next stop. We were supposed to stop masking by six o'clock, but we went on until around four in the morning. We went back to Felicia's house, had a good meal, and hit the street again.

Jerry Brock, Historian, Broadcaster, and Filmmaker

BORN: Texas, September 4, 1955

Interviewed at the Croissant d'Or Café, Ursuline Street, October 2002

I've always tried to be behind the scenes and supportive of the music and the New Orleans culture. I came here in 1976, to contribute to starting WWOZ radio; my brother Walter and I were both community radio activists.

I had been involved with Lorenzo Milam in a station called KCHU in Dallas, Texas. He gave us a choice of locations; we had already been involved in setting up new radio stations in Tampa, Florida, and Tulsa, Oklahoma. We chose New Orleans because it was in the South, where we were from. We knew of the music of Louis Armstrong, Fats Domino, Sidney Bechet, and Jelly Roll Morton; both my brother and I, from a very young age, were fanatics for literature and music of all kinds. The astounding thing, once we arrived in New Orleans, was that we had no idea that this musical tradition was a continuum of a much earlier tradition, with the people. It just hit us like a ton of bricks.

Within the first two weeks of being here, we'd met everybody. It floored us that this was a living, breathing culture that exists on a neighborhood-to-neighborhood basis. The original programming plans for WWOZ had been much more eclectic until we realized that no one was broadcasting to this community. The only time you heard any New Orleans music on the radio or TV back then was a little bit during Mardi Gras, and that was it. We realized there was a void to be filled.

We were hanging out with Professor Longhair, James Booker, and Huey "Piano" Smith, the Lastie family, all these other beautiful people. And Danny Barker had a big influence on me personally. In many ways, he was like a father figure to me.

Walter and I used to always joke that if we were to dedicate the programming of WWOZ to Garden District architecture, we'd never have problems raising money. But we realized that the important thing was to dedicate it to New Orleans music culture. At that time, the majority of that culture was being done by working-class people, as far as economics go.

When Danny saw the work we were putting into the project, he just opened his arms to us. Being the intellectual cat that he was, he really understood the struggle that we went through. The City of New Orleans and the archdiocese took us to federal court and tried to stop the radio station. Essentially 90.7 FM, where WWOZ exists on the dial, was the last frequency of any consequence. Their public statement was that they wanted to use that frequency for teaching students at the Notre Dame Seminary—religious broadcasting techniques and practices.

Lorenzo Milam was the founder of noncommercial radio in America—he lives in San Diego now. He'd been identified by the extreme right in America as the Antichrist. In 1973 he wrote what became known as the "Petition against God." He had spent all his time and energy and money building commercial radio, and he saw that religious broadcasting had the support and the wherewithal to open all these radio stations. They were taking up all the noncommercial frequencies that were available. He made a petition to the FCC [Federal Communication Commission] requesting a ninety-day freeze on allotting any new permits, to determine whether there should be a whole new frequency band for religious broadcasts. To this day, the FCC has never officially accepted the petition, but people are still organizing in communities to defeat it. My brother and I were identified with Lorenzo Milam, so once we got here, the Catholic Church wanted to stop us. They saw us being a part of this man who was against religious broadcasting. So that's the unstated reason why they took us to federal court.

The music doesn't have the depth it once had. Even though New Orleans is still considered one of the most musical cities in the world, it's only a fraction of what was here, when you really look at the thousands of jazz artists who emerged out of this community in the early part of the century. What happened here was a renaissance which has affected popular music all over the world since it occurred.

You could compare it to the Baroque renaissance in Austria, with the Bach family, Handel, all of them. That's why our dedication became having this New Orleans music recognized, not just as a fine art, but also as a great art. People like Kid Thomas and George Lewis and Danny Barker and the Barbarins—these people dedicated their lives to this music. That's one thing you feel in New Orleans today, that the sense of dedication isn't as great as it once was, that music isn't just something you do for a living, that it's a way of life. What sets this community apart from many other musical communities—it's because the music is a living, breathing continuum. It's a tradition that goes back to the founding of the city.

Danny Barker had returned from New York in the mid-sixties. He recognized that the music he loved and had grown up with was dying out. You had a few semiactive brass bands. The Olympia was really the only regular working brass band. The Eureka had died out. Floyd Anckle would pull the Majestic together for gigs from time to time; Doc Paulin always did certain parades every year, the Mount Moriah Missionary Baptist Church being one of them. But there wasn't much encouragement to young people to get involved.

I can't remember exactly how I first met Danny. I think he brought me to a jazz funeral around 1978. In a simplified way, it turned my world around. I'd heard of these things, but I'd no idea of the depth and the pathos and the tradition that musical funerals represented. By being with Danny, I was already a celebrity. The band was the Olympia. I met James Andrews Sr., the trumpet player's father, that day. Young James, who started the All Star Brass Band, began playing with Danny's Roots of Jazz Brass Band in the early eighties. After the funeral, James Senior needed a ride home, and he was living close to where Danny lived, four streets away, in the St. Bernard project. I gave them a ride, and then I went over to James's house in the projects and met his wife, Lois. At that time, young James couldn't have been more than six years old. I've had a friendship with James since that time—I still see him at least once a week.

All of these experiences emphasized to me the importance and significance of building this radio station and getting this music into the community through the media. There had been hundreds of people at this funeral; you could sense the importance of the event. These musical funerals and second line parades are much more important to the people who attend them than the Saints' games or Mardi Gras.

They're dedicated to doing that, and you can feel it. You hear the people moan, and cry, and see tears flowing, the solemnity of it, and at the same time, the celebration of it. I was greatly moved by that, and it motivated me to start hanging around the second lines. At that time, the only light-skinned people hanging around second lines were myself, Michael Smith the photographer, and Jules Cahn the entrepreneur. I wasn't writing a book, I wasn't taking photos, I wasn't making a film—I just hung out.

I got to meet all these beautiful people, whom I still have friendships with: the guys who went on to create the Dirty Dozen, Tuba Fats, Little James. I remember going to the first funeral little James Andrews played, when he was twelve years old: it was the funeral for his grandfather "Black Walter" Nelson. His sons were Papoose and Prince La La—Papoose had played guitar with Fats Domino.

We finally got on the air with WWOZ on December 4, 1980, and I started hanging out with James Andrews Sr. a lot. He was nicknamed "Twelve" because, as a crap shooter, he would always be able to hit double sixes: it's known as "boxcars" in the game of craps. James had around his neck two gold dice, with the two sixes aiming out, so you could see them. He organized and formed the High Rollers Social Aid and Pleasure Club. He's dedicated his life to the second line. That's the most important thing he has ever done, or will ever do: participate in that.

Into the seventies, there had been a slight revival of New Orleans music. A lot of great players were still alive who had been ignored by the media. Tipitina's club was opening uptown, WWOZ was getting together, and the Jazz Festival was becoming a worldwide event.

Certainly the media can exaggerate, misconstrue, and mislead. But with WWOZ, we had the people doing the programming themselves, having hands-on participation. After spending $50,000 on legal expenses, I got a call from an FCC commissioner on December 3, 1980. He said, "Can you be on the air?" Within twenty-four hours, we were broadcasting. It was amazing.

We were broadcasting out of a cinder-block transmitter shack on the Mississippi River. So there was no way our audience could reach us. This went on for about five months. I'd stay up all night making tapes, then drive out to the transmitter, sit there for ten hours a day, and run the tapes. It was pretty painful.

Then the people at Tipitina's allowed us to put a studio above their nightclub. The very first day we had a phone so people could reach us, Snooks Eaglin called us. He said, "I'm listening. I can hear it. Sounding good to me. Keep it going. I'm with y'all." I'm like, "Who is this?" He says, "This is Fird Eaglin." I said, "Can we put you on our mailing list?" He said, "I'll have to call you back. Let me ask my wife." Then the second day, David Lastie calls up, when we'd just played the very first recording he'd ever made. He had been driving in his car when he heard it, pulled over to a pay phone. He said, "This is David Lastie. I can't believe y'all got that record." Musicians just came out of the woodwork. Nobody had given them any attention in their own community. When my brother and I were running WWOZ, it was the only radio station in America that had a fifty-fifty black and white audience.

Walter and I worked for almost four years for not one dollar. We struggled. Both of us were working numerous part-time jobs and working twelve hours a day at the radio station. We finally started to get paid towards the end, but not much. That's why people like Danny Barker just embraced us. People in New Orleans figured we were either total idiots or insane millionaires with Texas oil fortunes. They didn't know we were truly idiots! It was through that dedication that the people gave us what we needed—the community built WWOZ with their sweat, their blood, their money. That's why it's as successful as it is today. That's what gave it its base.

Danny's love of the brass bands, and Leroy Jones and Tuba Fats, that's what made me close to those guys. He introduced me to Shannon Powell, Michael White, Lucien Barbarin. He realized that we shared a love of the music.

In 1980, we produced the first recording by the Dirty Dozen Brass Band. It wasn't released—I still have the master tapes. We did it solely so that we could have their music to play on the radio, and we played it constantly.

The first time I ever heard them was at Big Chief Jolly's funeral. Big Chief Jolly, George Landry, a wonderful barrelhouse piano player, in the style of Jack Dupree, was also the uncle of the Neville Brothers. He had really encouraged them to get into music. He was also the Big Chief of the Wild Tchoupitoulas Mardi Gras Indian tribe. His funeral was a big deal; it was a massive event. I think it was early 1979. I was recording the funeral—I had this little stereo recorder. The Olympia had played inside the church and led the casket out. There were lots of Indians; the Nevilles were there and the Meters, all beating tambourines. It was at a church uptown. The Dirty Dozen was there. It was a group that had just come together—you could hear that they were struggling with ideas within the framework of the music. They had not, at that point, progressed to where they were playing those incredible tight arrangements and riffs that they became known for, using the New Orleans second line tradition as a basis to jump off into any form of music they chose. They were all very talented musicians, but their ideas just hadn't crystallized yet.

It was obvious that they were rehearsing like crazy. Just a few months later, they started to perform once a week at a club called Daryl's. It's down in the Seventh Ward, on Tonti Street, between Conti and Rocheblave.

I'll never forget the first time I walked in there. I could barely get in—it was only a small black-owned barroom in a poor neighborhood. I mean, the place was just exploding. The band had been practicing, and they had figured out what they were going to do. The people were so exuberant—the floor was covered with people, rolling on the floor! I was afraid to step on them. And there were at least six men in their sixties and seventies dancing on top of the bar. This is what the Fairview band and the Hurricane Brass Band had been leading up to—the Dirty Dozen had renewed this music to speak to the contemporary New Orleans community. The people were going wild. Going to Daryl's became the weekly ritual.

At Daryl's on Thursday night, it was just an explosion of spirit. They would serve red beans. There was not one person who was not dancing. Everybody was moving—the music was moving them. The more the people moved, it moved the music even more. People were taking their clothes off—the place was crammed, it was so hot (there was no air conditioning), they were sweating. In between sets, everybody would pile outside, just to cool off before going back for the next set. The Dozen was a complete show—there was no break from one song to the next. They'd play three hour-long sets, and if they felt good, maybe longer. Each set was like a complete symphony—that was something new.

I interviewed Gregory Davis in the mid-eighties and asked him to explain what did the Dozen do that's different. They stepped outside the traditional boundaries. The first song they did that the old guys criticized them for was "Night Train." They were willing

Dirty Dozen Brass Band, Jackson Square, 1986 (Kirk Joseph, Efrem Towns, Lionel Batiste Jr., Gregory Davis, Jennell Marshall, Roger Lewis) *Photo by Marcel Joly*

to bring in material that meant something to their own lives and experience. In many ways, it's no different than what had happened before: brass bands in New Orleans have always adapted the music that was popular in their time. In that sense, they were part of that same tradition.

There were other people who contributed to that. Tuba Fats had recorded "Mardi Gras in New Orleans" with the Olympia Brass Band; Leroy Jones, "Leroy's Special" with the Hurricane Brass Band; they were all leading in this direction, you could feel that.

The Dirty Dozen brought that tendency to fruition, and they dedicated themselves to it, more than anybody else had previously. They rehearsed and Frog Joseph had a big influence on them—they rehearsed in his backyard, and he would mentor them and their sound as a brass band. He wasn't against them taking the music in new directions, but it was like, "If you're going to do it, do it right." He influenced them in that way—correct harmony, counterpoint, rhythmic interest, that kind of thing. It helped them create a big sound, big chords.

People didn't pay attention to what was going on back then. Whenever I recorded the Dozen, I couldn't pay them, but they were just thrilled that anybody was taking any notice of them, especially someone who was connected with the music business. One of my contributions to brass bands was to make them understand, early on, the importance of having your business together. I did the first press kit for the Dirty Dozen and helped them to present themselves professionally. We produced a calendar for them, and I arranged a concert for them, which was the first time they had played in a white club, Tipitina's. That introduced them to a whole new audience—that was in 1982. They hadn't made any official recordings by that time.

They emerged from this deeply rooted community tradition that included the Baby Dolls and the Original Sixth Ward Dirty Dozen Kazoo Band. I paraded with the Baby Dolls on the last time they went out: that was Mardi Gras Day, 1981. It was a Mardi Gras tradition; the Dirty Dozen kind of grew out of it. Benny Jones was around, Uncle Lionel Batiste. It was his family that were the nucleus of that Mardi Gras group. It was a real folk movement within the community.

Jenell Marshall, the snare drummer, would organize these parades where all the men would dress as drag queens, all out marching down the street, and they'd just be beating on tubs and bottles—they just did it for fun and the love of life. If you're from New Orleans, and you have any sort of social conscience, you realize that classism and racism are very deep rooted. Not for everyone, but historically. These people in the black neighborhoods had learned for centuries how to enjoy life, amongst the greatest repression. They have really made life special, and they have made it their own. People that are forgotten today were part of that scene: Andrew Green the drummer, Cyrille Salvant the trumpet player.

The Dirty Dozen grew out of all that culture; it wasn't as if they were created in a vacuum. They made a musical climate in which it was possible for the Rebirth Brass Band to exist. When Danny Barker and the Reverend Darby put the Fairview Baptist band together, not only were the brass bands dying out, but the second line clubs had sort of ceased to exist as well. When the Dozen exploded musically, it gave the impetus to clubs to start parading again. Of course, the Olympia band played the older, traditional club parades, but people turned out to the Dozen's second line parades in masses—more so than they do today. Today, an average four-hour second line parade is probably witnessed by around eight thousand people. But back then, you might have around five thousand people actually following the parade. The tune that finished every performance was "Feet Don't Fail Me Now." That became the anthem of the street.

People romanticize about the Tremé and its importance in the history of jazz, but there were many neighborhoods that were important. But certainly for the revival of the seventies and eighties, Tremé was very significant. It's gone through tremendous changes in the last fifteen years. The real estate has skyrocketed because it's such a historic area. People realized that there were all these incredibly beautiful houses there.

JERRY BROCK, HISTORIAN, BROADCASTER, AND FILMMAKER 101

The Rebirth headquarters was on North Villere Street between St. Philip and Ursulines. That's where Philip and Keith Frazier lived with their mother, Barbara. As kids, they had witnessed the Dirty Dozen, the Chosen Few, all of that.

In a way, it was the newfound freedom of civil rights that gave the youth the impetus to have freedom in the music. There's a parallel between that and the way emancipation spawned so many brass bands after the Civil War.

In the 1960s, the NAACP tried to stop the second lines. It wasn't that they had bad intentions; it's just that they felt that it was a bit of a throwback, and it was time to move on. Harold Dejan and Danny Barker stood up to them and said, "This is valuable. This is a part of the history of our people."

I used to call Danny Barker "the last sidewalk intellectual." He would hang out with the brothers on the street corner, drink a beer, shoot the shit, smoke a joint, whatever was happening. He could discuss history, art, world music—his interests were not confined to his music that became known as jazz.

The Rebirth, being young kids, it was all the most exciting thing they saw. The majority of them were going to Joseph Clark High School, so they got together. Allison Miner, who later became their manager, really helped turn the Rebirth into a world-class band. I saw potential in them, and I wanted to help them develop. Allison was producing a jazz series at the Contemporary Arts Center. I asked Allison as a favor, "Look, I'm working with these kids—it would really mean a lot, they've never played on a stage—could they get up and do just one song before your concert starts?" She's like, "OK, Jerry, as a favor to you, I'll do it." So we showed up at the right time, got on stage, and started playing. After maybe a minute and a half of "Lord, Lord, Lord" Allison stomped out on the stage and scolded me for bringing a group like this that was not ready to be presented to any audience and told us to get out. She was a very strong-minded woman. It was really ironic that, ten years later, she thought they were the greatest thing since sliced bread!

Round about the same time, I had them play for this function for WWOZ in Armstrong Park. Kermit [Ruffins] was up there playing, and some guy came up to me and said, "That's the worst trumpet player I ever heard in my life. Why are you letting him play?" Now, Kermit's still not the greatest in the world, but he's working regularly, and he's developed a lot. I mean, somebody has to encourage emerging talent.

In 1984, Danny Barker decided to organize new workshops—he was going to organize another children's group. He started a band called the Roots of Jazz Brass Band, and James Andrews was the leader of that. He couldn't have been more than eight or nine at that time. Nicholas Payton was in that group. A lot of the band personnel were members of the Andrews family—"Peanut," Darnell, "Buster."

Within a year, James realized, "Hey, we got something here." So they formed their own group, James Andrews and the All Stars. Shortly after that, Lois, his mother, rented a building on Governor Nicholls and Marais Street. It became known as "the Hall." Tuba Fats lived upstairs; I lived around the corner. It became the spot. Every Monday, we would barbecue out there, the band would perform, Tuba would show them how the music went. Clark Terry would come by if he was in the neighborhood.

The Hall was covered with murals of brass bands. James had sat at the feet of Kid Thomas and Teddy Riley. As a kid, he really did try to absorb this New Orleans sound. When James was around fourteen, he was playing in this place called the Tremé Lounge. I was in there, sharing a drink with Harold Dejan. I asked Harold who he thought James sounded like. Harold said he reminded him of Kid Howard when he was young.

In about 1986, it was a special time. Tuba had the Chosen Few, the Tuxedo were still working, there was the Olympia, the Dirty Dozen were out on the road, there was the Pinstripe Brass Band uptown, Floyd Anckle had reorganized the Majestic, and the Rebirth.

I was kind of an outsider looking in, but I became an insider. I didn't think about it—I was with my friends. The friendship wasn't all about the music. It extended to "If you've got a flat tire, let's help you fix it. If you need to move, let's help each other move."

Most of the people today who participate in the tradition really don't know what it's about—all they know is their own personal experience. There's over forty-four second line parades annually now. That's more than there's ever been.

THE BACKSTREET CULTURAL MUSEUM

A POWERHOUSE OF KNOWLEDGE

2002 — 2003 Second Line Parade Schedule

(Dates are subject to change without notice)

SEPTEMBER 2002

BLACK MEN OF LABOR (D) — Sept. 1, 2002
YOUNG MEN OLYMPIAN (U) — Sept. 8, 2002
ORIGINAL JOLLY BUNCH (U) — Sept. 16, 2002
YOUNG MEN OLYMPIAN (U) — Sept. 22, 2002
STEP-N-STYLE (U) — Sept. 29, 2002

OCTOBER 2002

LADY SEQUENCE (U) — Oct. 6, 2002
ORIGINAL PRINCE OF WALES (U) — Oct. 13, 2002
FAMILY TIES (?) — Oct. 19, 2002
POPULAR LADIES (D) — Oct. 20, 2002
N.O. EAST STEPPERS (D) — Oct. 20, 2002
AVENUE STEPPERS (U) — Oct. 27, 2002
SUGAR HILL GANG (U) — Oct. 27, 2002

NOVEMBER 2002

BACKSTREET CULTURAL MUSEUM SALUTE
TO ALL SAINTS DAY (D) — Nov. 1, 2002
MONEY WASTERS (D) — Nov. 3, 2002
MEN OF THE NEW MILLENUIM (U) — Nov. 3, 2002
UNDEFEATED DIVAS (U) — Nov. 10, 2002
SUDAN (D) — Nov. 10, 2002
NO LIMIT (U) — Nov. 16, 2002
ORIGINAL LADY BUCKJUMPERS (U) — Nov. 24, 2002
NINE TIMES (T-GIVING) (D) — Nov. 28, 2002

DECEMBER 2002

WESTBANK STEPPERS (W) — Dec. 1, 2002
DUMAINE GANG (D) — Dec. 1, 2002
LADY& MEN ROLLERS (U) — Dec. 29, 2002
BIG 9 (D) — Dec. 29, 2000

JANUARY 2003

SECOND LINE JAMMERS (D) — Jan. 5, 2003
CTC STEPPERS (U) — Jan. 12, 2003

CARROLTON (U) — Jan. 19, 2003

FEBRUARY 2003

DIVINE LADIES (U) — Feb. 16, 2003

**MARDI GRAS PARADE SEASON STARTS
FRIDAY, FEBRUARY 21, 2003 THROUGH
TUESDAY, MARCH 4, 2003 (no second lines
during this time).**

MARCH 2003

TREME STEPPERS (D) — Mar. 9, 2003
DEVESTATION (U) — Mar. 9, 2003
SINGLE MEN (U) — Mar. 16, 2003
SUPER SUNDAY (D) — Mar. ? 2003
SUPER SUNDAY (U) — Mar. ? 2003
REVOLUTION (D) — Mar. 23, 2003
NANDI (U) — Mar. 30, 2003

APRIL 2002

JAZZ FEST / SUNDAY TO REMEMBER — Apr. 6
PIOLET TOWN ROLLERS (U) — Apr. 12, 2003
PIGEON TOWN STEPPERS (U) — Apr. 13, 2003
OLD & NEW STYLE (D) — Apr. 20, 2003
ORIGINAL BIG "7" (D) — Apr. 27, 2003

MAY 2003

SINGLE LADIES (U) — May 11, 2003

BACKSTREET CULTURAL MUSEUM
1116 St. Claude
(Between Governor Nicholls & Ursulines)
New Orleans, LA 70116
504-522-4806 / backstreetculturalmuseum.org
Hours: 10am — 5pm, Tuesday — Saturday
Key: (U) Uptown, (D) Downtown,
(W) Westbank

Rebirth Brass Band

The Rebirth Brass Band

Maple Leaf Bar, Oak Street, Tuesday night
home of the Rebirth Brass Band
Photo by Barry Martyn

In the early summer of 1983, a group of high school musicians left their first-ever gig, which was at the Sheraton Hotel on Canal Street. They didn't feel like going home, it was still early in the evening, and they decided to try their luck playing for tips in the French Quarter. That spontaneous decision led to the formation of the Rebirth Brass Band, and for those founding members, music was to be the only job they ever had.

They were taking local jobs and playing in the Quarter every day when they came to the notice of Allison Miner, whose close involvement with the new bands of the time accelerated interest in their music. She had bonded with the music community while working at Tulane's Hogan Jazz Archive with Quint Davis, and she had noticed how fickle public tastes threw good musicians out of work. In a sense, she almost became the conscience of the Jazz Festival, prompting the organizers to put older musicians like Tuts Washington and Professor Longhair back in the public eye.

After a few years living in Cleveland and New York, she returned to New Orleans in the late eighties and began working with the Rebirth—she had been turned on to the street music scene by photographer Jules Cahn. She persuaded Quint Davis to book the band in Europe and set up a deal with Rounder Records.

All of this was more than fifteen years ago, but the Rebirth has lost none of its energy and drive. They've been resident at the Maple Leaf Bar on Oak Street for at least twelve years.

Their speciality is doing a forty-minute set without any pauses between the songs—just a few bars of bass horn and drum to set the groove, and straight into the next number. After twenty years, they're still working hard.

Philip Frazier III, Bass Horn

BORN: New Orleans, February 10, 1966

Founder and leader of the Rebirth Brass Band

Interviewed at 3621 Burgundy Street, November 2002

Photo by Emile Martyn

I have two brothers who are musicians: Keith is the bass drummer with the Rebirth Brass Band, and my baby brother, Kerwin James, is the tuba player with the New Birth. Kerwin has my mother's last name. Cié Frazier is my great uncle. I started playing music because of my mother—she played gospel piano in the Christian Mission Church on North Robertson, in the Tremé. My brothers and sister used to sing in the choir there.

When I got in grade school, I started playing trombone. My brother started playing baritone horn, and we used to go to church sometimes to play with my mother. That's where it started, but in high school, that's where it really took off. I attended Joseph S. Clark High School; so did my brother Keith. The band director at the time was David Harris; he was a trumpet player. Also my mother had been to Clark School. Milton Batiste had been at Clark with my father; they were in the first class.

I played the usual high school stuff. Marching in Mardi Gras parades, football games, stuff like that. We would play regular military marches for the most part. At that time, I was playing trombone. Then, at Clark, they started to run out of tuba players. During the eighties, there weren't so many young people taking it up. I was really small and skinny, and I decided to start playing tuba. Everybody thought I was joking! But I knew I could pick it up pretty good. I took a tuba home and practiced every day. I used to sleep with it: my mother thought I was crazy.

I was also the band captain of the school band. We had this band parent booster club. One of the parents asked me to get a brass band together to come and play at a function. I got a group of guys together: Kermit Ruffins (because he was in the band with me); Reginald Steward, the trombone player, who's now with the New Birth Brass Band; Cheryl McKay on clarinet—she now plays with a reggae band; and Dimitri Smith, old

Smitty D, on tuba; and I played trombone. We practiced, got some material together, and did a function at the Sheraton Hotel on Canal Street. We were still sixteen and seventeen years old, and they were serving alcoholic beverages. That meant that after we played, we had to leave.

I had seen Keith Anderson playing with the Young Men Brass Band, and they were hustling in the French Quarter every day for tips. So I had the idea to do the same—it was only about ten o'clock at night. Dimitri Smith was in the union, so he couldn't go down there. I said, "OK, give me the tuba." I went down there with the rest of the guys, and we put a box down for tips. We made some money, and everybody wanted to do the same thing the next day. Everybody slept at my house, and we went back to the Quarter the next day. This was the summer of 1983—it was just something good to do.

We had listened to the Preservation Hall Jazz Band and the Olympia Brass Band on records. That's where we got our first music from. Tunes like "The Saints" and "Second Line." We just happened to be in the right place at the right time, as things happened. We were playing in the French Quarter, and then we got our first paying gig, playing for the Zulu Club at their picnic.

The tunes came out sounding different from the Olympia, but that was just a natural thing. By us all coming from a high school band, we were powerful. That was when the rap and hip-hop thing started, around the same time as we did. We heard those things on the radio, and we wanted to incorporate them into our repertoire. It worked real well, because we were the youngest band in the city, apart from the Young Men, but they had started breaking up. So nobody else was doing it.

The Dirty Dozen is one of my favorite bands. One night, my stepfather (he was in a second line club) drove me up to Second and Saratoga and parked outside the Glasshouse. We could hear the Dirty Dozen through the door. That was in the late seventies, and it made me want to get into brass bands. I first heard them play again at my cousin's funeral, and that's the first time I heard them play "Blackbird Special." I can remember it like it was yesterday—it was on Dumaine and North Robertson. I had never heard anything like that before in my life. It was phenomenal. They were a big influence. When we got old enough, we used to go hang in the Glasshouse every Monday night. One of my favorite records is the Dozen's "Feet Don't Fail Me Now" album, when Mr. Benny Jones was in the band. We call that album "the bible."

The Rebirth plays a kind of unorganized organized music. We didn't write anything down; we just had a basic formation. We'd start with the tuba and then bring in the melody, and everybody else would play around it—that was the whole thing. In the past, brass bands would introduce the tunes with the drum, but when we were on the street, the parades would have such a vibe, the music couldn't stop. So I'd tell the drums to keep going, and I'd bring in another song on tuba, like setting the groove.

My two favorite tuba players are Kirk Joseph and Tuba Fats—they're top of my list. And I love the sound of my brother Kerwin. He's a big guy, but he's got a sweet sound. I just left him; he's going to Brazil tomorrow with the New Birth.

Our success didn't happen overnight, but in the nineteen years we've been together, it's been a phenomenal life. People first noticed us on the parades, because we would play twenty-five songs in a row without stopping. That started a new trend. As we got more into playing the hip-hop tunes we heard on records, we started to write more of our own material. Everybody had an input to that.

We had a few connections, one of whom was Ice Cube Slim—Dan Untermyer. He got us to Europe, to a couple of North Sea festivals in Holland, and to Japan. Then a lot of stuff in Germany, and then a lot of stuff around the States. We were doing pretty well traveling. But where the breakthrough really came was when we did the song "Do Watcha Wanna," which was written by Kermit Ruffins and me and Keith Anderson. We recorded it first in 1986 with Milton Batiste and again in 1989 for Rounder Records. They put the song in a record rotation on a hip-hop radio station. The songs being broadcast were in competition with each other, and "Do Watcha Wanna" was the number one for eight weeks in a row. That really did it. We were number one, in competition with Luther VanDross and O.J. It really opened doors for us.

I first met Allison Miner—God bless her—when we were playing a gig by the municipal auditorium. People had told me about her and how she had worked with Quint Davis when they started the Jazz Festival. She had been in Cleveland but had just come back to New Orleans. She came up to us and said, "I heard about you guys—I have a gig I want you to do." She took us to Baton Rouge, and after that she loved the band so much she became our manager. That lasted about five years. It was a great connection; she was really good for the band. She took us to another level. She kind of taught me the ropes, in a business way. I give her credit for all that side that people don't see. How to get a tax ID, how to get incorporated, all of that. I still miss her.

Among the upcoming brass bands, I would vote the Lil' Stooges and the Hot 8 Brass Band. I mean, they're patterning themselves after the Rebirth, but they're the new generation. They're doing parades, playing in clubs, and now they've started recording. They're the newest groups that are coming up, and in a way, it's due to us.

Right now, listening to everybody, they're still following what we're doing. The only difference is we live it. What I mean by that is we've really lived Rebirth twenty-four *hours a day since day one. We opened doors for a lot of other bands. When we were out in the French Quarter playing for tips every day, we didn't have anything else but the Rebirth Brass Band. But a lot of younger musicians now have to have day jobs and also be in a brass band. That's all I've ever done. We're getting ready to do our twenty-year anniversary record next year; I'm trying to get everybody back for that: Kermit, Keith Anderson—a big reunion. It's been kind of like Rebirth University, the number of people that came out of the band and are doing something.*

When we do something without chord changes, we call that simple music—the bass horn just stays on a set line, and it makes it danceable music. When people want to go out and dance, they don't care about chord changes. What they want to hear is a hook. With a good hook, they always recognize that song, and it makes them feel like dancing. If music is too complicated, people don't dance, they go and sit down. We try and get them up to dance. They say, "Hey, I like that line," and it moves them. We put the bass line down first, and everything else goes on top.

Sometimes on the street, I think of these things, sometimes I think them up at home— if you can dance off it, we can work with it. We want people to be dancing all the time. If we don't want them dancing, we do music with all the changes and stuff. But those simple things get the crowd dancing, get everybody to rowdy up—it works good. We're still playing for the younger generation, but we're better playing for people around our own age, because they know us from when we started.

The competitions of the bands on the street are great, but it's more because that's what people want to see. Sometimes we do it to make the parade more entertaining, a bit of friendly competition. Let me put it like this: if we were a football team, our competition record would be a hundred and twenty. A hundred wins, twenty losses. Right now, the biggest threat is the Hot 8 Brass Band. They're the new guys coming up, and they're hungry.

My dream is I would love to win a Grammy with a brass band. But if I had to do it again for no money, I would, because I love doing it.

Keith Frazier, Bass Drum

BORN: New Orleans, October 3, 1968

Founding member of the Rebirth Brass Band

Interviewed at 3621 Burgundy Street, November 2002

Photo by Emile Martyn

I came into music by watching my brother Philip playing when I was in elementary school. It seemed something that was fun to do, so I wanted to do it too.

He was playing trombone in the James Lewis Elementary School. When I got to be his age, I wanted to get in the junior high school marching band. I was playing snare drum at the time, but they said I was too small to play drums, so they switched me to baritone horn. I carried on with the baritone horn all the way up to college. I was just playing drums on the side, really, until the Rebirth officially formed.

I had started snare drum by playing around the house: my brother Philip used to bring these guys round to play in the garage, so I said, "I guess I'll play drums." So when I got to school, that was my first choice. Drums had been a long-term hobby, but when the Rebirth started, they needed someone to play drums. I said, "OK, I'll give it a shot." It worked!

The Rebirth's been a great experience—traveling the world, playing for all kinds of important people, taking us to places we never thought it would. It was just a hobby, something to do during the course of the summer; it's turned into a full time job. We've played for George [Herbert Walker] Bush when he came down for the National Republican Convention, when he was president.

The bass drum's the most important thing in the band. We always say, "If the bass is not knocking, the band is not rocking." So the bass drum has to be doing what it's doing. Some people don't understand that; they don't see it, they don't even know what it is. You can have people dancing just to the bass drum.

It takes a little time to develop an understanding with a snare drummer; myself and the Rebirth's current snare drummer have been working together for over ten years now—that's Ajay Mallery. He took a three-year hiatus from the band, and we used dif-

ferent guys. But with Ajay, we really don't talk, we just play.

Our first snare drummer was "Eyes" [Kenneth Austin]. He and I worked together for quite some time. He was one of the first people to play with the snare off all the time, kind of gives the drum a timbale sound. He was just trying something different—like when you're a kid, you're always experimenting.

We were real close friends—we knew each other from high school. Our families knew each other, and even when we weren't playing music, he used to hang out at our house all the time. It's important to get on well with the other guy. If you hate the snare drummer, it's not going to come off. Even if you're not friends, you try not to have any conflict with them.

When I first started playing the bass drum, I would listen to Mr. Benny Jones. He was with the Dirty Dozen at the time. The album they had out was "Feet Don't Fail Me Now." I would listen to it all the time. I kind of picked up on a lot of what he was doing. He was playing more of a straight beat—one, two, three, four. That was the style, but it was different from what the traditional drummers were doing. It was modern, it was cool. I liked it. I don't know if the other guys in the band did, and I kind of picked up on it. I listened to the guys from the Chosen Few Brass Band. They were from uptown. They were one of the funkiest brass bands around. The first time I heard them was in the French Quarter.

I just picked up on it, and added my thing. What I try to do is like continuous bass drum—there's always a beat, always a sound coming from the bass drum. There wouldn't be a lot of spaces. With traditional bass drums, there's a lot of syncopation, and so you get a lot of spaces. What I was trying to do was not have any spaces, like with a heartbeat that doesn't stop. If you keep that going, the feel for the dancers dancing off the bass drum will always be going. It's kind of like the Rebirth style—it's always moving. Like in high school marching band music, the bass drum is marking the tempo, so it's like a one, two, three, four beat, never syncopated. We try and keep it filled in. I think we invented something there.

Most of the time, I play four beats on the cymbal. It's for the benefit of the horn players—if they can't hear the bass drum, they kind of lose track of the time, and the tempo will go down. It was a conscious effort to do something different. Some of the other bands, the drummers are syncopating a lot, and they're playing offbeats. It gets kind of boring if you're doing a parade for four hours. But if you see us on a second line, it's fast, and it's moving; there's never any space anywhere—it's always busy.

I have the bass drum muffled because otherwise the beats will carry over and run into each other. You muffle the drum, and that gives you that definition. Not so with traditional style: they could let the drum ring, because of the space.

One night, the thing I play the cymbal with, I lost it, and one of the band said, "Hey man, I have a screwdriver in my car!" I said, "Let me try that." The metal on metal was a pretty good sound, sort of like water hitting the ocean—a splash, as opposed to a stick, which is a clear sound. Then everyone started playing with screwdrivers. They were like, "Well, we saw you doing it, so we figured it was something cool to do."

I think it's great when other bands copy our style—it's like flattery. I'm glad people like it. I never had specific private lessons—I just picked up most of what I know from messing around and listening to other drummers. I try to tune to the B-flat from the tuba. Most of our tunes are in B-flat—it's a marching key, it sounds loud, so it carries on the street.

The Rebirth thing seems to be getting bigger and bigger—we play more in the United States than we ever did. In the beginning, we were always traveling to Europe, because they have a lot of festivals there, and the people seemed to appreciate the music, more than home. Then it started picking up in the United States, and we travel the States now more than ever before. My favorite place in the world to play is probably Amsterdam—it seems a lot like New Orleans.

I'll sometimes have a drink when I'm not on stage, but I prefer to stay sober when I'm playing; otherwise things can get sloppy. Because it's always busy, there's a lot going on. We do a lot of improvisation—we might change the head of a song right on the spot. You have to remember a lot. Sometimes somebody forgets, some guys will be playing one thing, some guys another. But if you do it almost every day, you already know, like, "We usually do this right here." And we do different versions; according to what the drums are doing, the guys know which one we're going to do.

Sometimes it just happens; I don't know how the horn players do it. We're playing, someone is talking a solo, no one knows what's coming next, and the horn players are just talking, and they just come in on a riff together. And Philip gives a lot of signals from the bass horn.

It's never written down; we never know what songs we're going to play—it just happens. The music's just different things we hear—there's different age groups in the band, people listen at different stuff. People might come in and want to do, for instance, a Curtis Mayfield song. They come in and give Philip the bass part, and the horn players figure it out. Although everyone in the band can read charts, we don't like to do it; people feel it more without.

The music was different, it was angrier, back in the late eighties. When you're dealing with synthetic drugs, you're dealing with a different kind of musician, and everything's just different.

Rebirth Brass Band, 1987 (Kermit Ruffins, Keith Frazier, Keith Anderson, John "Prince" Gilbert)
Photo by Marcel Joly

It's more mellow now. You get a different type of feeling in the city, and the music's different. I tell people that what the brass bands are playing now isn't even close to what we were doing ten years ago. Our band is still good. But when we had Kermit Ruffins, Derek Wiley—the band we have now couldn't touch that band. Most of us were the same age; we came up playing the French Quarter together.

We would come up with songs—nobody ever called a background, it was so much easier. Nowadays, younger guys don't really understand the format of our music—they can't feel it. Like seventies grooves and stuff, they don't understand it, because they're so young. They're more into a hip-hop thing. Hip-hop music only has two sections, A and B. In the early eighties, we would do like A, B, C, D: it's different. I think this newer thing takes more than it adds. There's less music—it's more vocal-led than actual playing.

Sometimes we do certain songs—it's like, "I don't want to do that song. It's just not real music." But we have younger people in the audience at the Maple Leaf, and they seem to enjoy it, because that's the music they hear on TV. I must be getting old. When I started, I was fourteen; I'm thirty-four now. I've seen so many changes in the music. When we do second lines, people are just dancing to the drums. I would say the horns are just not happening—they could just take a holiday, go and sit down somewhere.

Most of the bands coming up now, they're really not doing anything that we haven't already done. The quality's going down, it's not going up. I mean, at one time, we used to play traditional songs at the Maple Leaf. We don't do that anymore. When we started, the Olympia Brass Band was still doing second line parades—they don't do that now. The tempo of songs at second lines now is superfast.

The Dirty Dozen was the band that inspired us—we always used to go to the Glasshouse on Monday night. We wanted to emulate what they were doing. Their music is different from ours—we call it "New York." It's fast, it's clean; the New Orleans feel is more laid back. After the Dirty Dozen stopped doing second lines, it was just the Rebirth for nearly ten years. There were some other bands doing it, but they weren't really organized bands like we were.

I tell the younger bands now, "Everything you're doing, we already did it—you sound like you're copying the Rebirth." We're in a band called Forgotten Souls; it's a mixture of guys from other bands, and we try to do something different. We use the bass and snare drums along with a set drum player. It's pretty much a stage brass band. I don't really know what you could do that's different—I know we haven't covered everything. There's something else out there, but it's up to someone else to find it.

Someone like Shamar Allen (he's our newest trumpet player), he's more of a straight-ahead jazz player, whereas Glen Andrews is more street, and "Kabuki" [Derrick Shezbie] is like a mixture of jazz and street. We have three different styles of trumpet playing. "Street" is more improvisation than jazz—you're doing a lot of stuff that you can't do in jazz. If you're playing jazz in the key of B-flat, you can't start playing in the key of A, because it's not going to fit, whereas in street, you can be playing a B-flat when the note's supposed to be B. You know it's wrong, but you can squeeze it in there. Or, on a scale, you can play a D when you're supposed to be playing an F—it's not actually right. In jazz, you have to play the chords correctly for the song to be right. But in street you can play outside the chords—it can sound good if everyone's doing it. You get one horn playing jazz and another playing street, it can be like a train wreck. But people say, "Sounds pretty good!" if it comes off. As a musician, you know it's wrong, but you do it anyway. One of the younger guys from the Lil' Stooges is saying to us, "Man, y'all playing some kind of chords!" We're like, "Look, man, you're on the street. Ain't nobody worried about what kind of chords y'all playing—just play." If people are dancing, it's not wrong.

Keith "Wolf" Anderson, Trombone and Bass Horn

BORN: Chicago, July 18, 1964

Played with the Young Men Brass Band (originating from the Tambourine and Fan Club),
the Rebirth Brass Band, the Dirty Dozen Brass Band, the Regal Brass Band, and the Olympia
Brass Band; currently freelancing

Interviewed at the Crescent City Brewhouse, Decatur Street, September 2001

Keith Anderson, Copenhagen

Photo by Peter Nissen

I was born in Chicago. My parents were from here, but my daddy had moved to Chicago before I was born. The family didn't move back to New Orleans until I was nine years old.

That's when I first heard kids my age playing on the street. Man, that tripped me out. Right there, I knew what I was going to do. I knew I had to be a musician. Like, even today, my daddy runs a trucking business, and my brothers and sisters all work for him—I guess it makes me kind of the black sheep, but I couldn't do all that sitting behind a desk, you know?

When we got back to New Orleans, I attended Bell Junior High. The musical director was Mr. Richardson; he started me out on trumpet with the school band. After I'd been playing for a couple of years, I went over by the Tambourine and Fan Club. That's a social club for young people, over on Claiborne, run by Mr. Jerome Smith. As well as sports activities, they had a little brass band, and I started playing trumpet with them. Later on, the Tambourine and Fan band went out on their own—they were working under the name of the Young Men Brass Band. We were all still at high school.

Remember I said that the young kids playing on the street was my first inspiration? It was around this time that I came across my second—Anthony "Tuba Fats" Lacen. I never learned anything about formal harmony—as far as I'm concerned, if Tuba does it, it's right, and if he doesn't, it's probably wrong.

He is the MAN! I heard him in Jackson Square, and I couldn't believe it—he is just so good. Tuba says his inspiration on bass was Wilbert Tillman. Of course, he plays a little more modern than Tillman, and I play a little more modern than Tuba. That was the cause of me taking up bass horn. He plays with such passion and feeling, and that's the way I play too. How you going to play what's in you if you don't give it 100 percent of yourself? Ninety percent isn't enough. I say to other musicians, "If you don't give the music everything you've got, why should an audience give you anything at all? I mean, why should they hire you?"

To me, playing music isn't about money. Obviously, you have to take care of business, but when I go on a gig, I like to do that first. It only takes five minutes, and then my mind is free to concentrate on the reason I'm there in the first place—playing music.

Anyway, to get back to the story—I had a little part-time job when I was in high school, and I was coming home from work one night when I heard the sound of a band coming from a house. I went in there, and it was Philip Frazier, Keith Frazier, Kermit Ruffins—what later became the Rebirth. They were playing sort of high school music, from charts they had got at school. I said to them, "Man, y'all sound good. You should play jazz, make yourself some money." They all laughed at me! What they didn't know was that I was a musician. What they also didn't know was that I always used to like to mess with other guy's horns, at high school and in the Tambourine and Fan band.

So I had some experience of playing trombone, bass drum, snare drum—I couldn't play them well, but I knew what to do. And of course I already played trumpet and bass horn. That's how I was able to help the other guys and show them what to do. Of course, Philip Frazier was the tuba player, so I had to switch horns again—this time to trombone. I love it—you have to be so precise, and I love a challenge. But when you got that right, the trombone is the most expressive of instruments. My favorite trombone player is Wendell Eugene.

So we started to get it together and work in the French Quarter every day—the full eight-piece band, which is what it had become. Sure, we made a few dollars, but more important, we improved a lot by playing together so much, and it gave us exposure. At that time, it wasn't called the Rebirth. Those guys called it the Group.

There was a guy, a rehabilitated convict, who was trying to help the community. He wasn't a rich man, but he had a job, and he used his earnings to fund a meeting place for ex-convicts, to counsel them from his own experience and help them get their lives back together. He heard us in the Quarter, and he used to hire us to play at this meetinghouse, to raise funds and gain publicity. Now, the name of this place was Re Birth, and that's where the band got its name.

Speaking of names, those guys gave me my nickname, which as you know is "Wolf."

Man, I really did not like that at first. It was because of how I had my hair at that time. Often guys had like naturals, but my hair hung straight down the back, like an Indian or something. And I had a lot of facial hair, sideburns, moustache, everything. So they called me "Wolf." I hated the name, but it stuck, and I'm used to it now.

A guy called "Ice Cube" [Dan Untermyer] first brought us over to Europe—I don't know his right name. He just heard us on the street in the Quarter and thought we might be popular overseas. We went to England, Germany, and Austria. That trip changed everything for me, for all of us. As a black man, as a musician, every way: we were so well treated, and the people were so enthusiastic. They really appreciated us.

Meanwhile, the band got hooked up with Allison Miner for representation. I think she was a little bit unused to the ways of business. Kermit Ruffins, Philip Frazier, and I had come up with a song called "Do Watcha Wanna." Allison Miner got Philip Frazier on his own and got him to put her name on the song. The thing is, the song did really well. We got our money eventually—we didn't really have to fight for it, but we didn't get it until just before Allison Miner died, so it was a long wait. By this time we were working all the time, with foreign trips every year, record dates, local jobs, etc.

Then Kirk Joseph left the Dirty Dozen, and they asked me to join on tuba. I've always loved playing bass horn, and I was probably the only one in New Orleans who could have done that job.

I stayed with them about a year and a half. I only recorded with them once—that was the Jelly Roll Morton album. It was the record company's idea to do those tunes. Roger Lewis and Greg Davis more or less ran things between them in that band. They commissioned Wardell Quezergue to write the charts. I remember the bass score was just a simple "oom-pah" part. They said, "Don't play it like that. Spice it up a little." So that's what I did.

After a while, there was a big reshuffle and I went back with the Rebirth. We were doing some recording at Milton Batiste's house, and he hired me for the Olympia when Edgar Smith couldn't make it. Harold Dejan was still singing with the band at this point, but he wasn't playing anymore. That makes me the only musician in New Orleans to play with the city's three top bands, the Rebirth, the Dirty Dozen, and Dejan's Olympia.

Milton fired me from the Olympia for missing a job. I had lent my horn to a friend to do an afternoon parade, and he didn't bring it back until midnight. So that's how I missed the Sunday night job at Preservation Hall.

After a while, the Rebirth and I parted company for the second time. I was working with a lot of different bands, and they said, "You're supposed to be with us. If people see you with all these bands, it makes us look cheap. It makes it look as though you need the money." I said, "I do need the money." So that was the end of that.

KEITH "WOLF" ANDERSON, TROMBONE AND BASS HORN 119

Kermit at Vaughan's, October 31, 2002

Vaughan's Bar and Grill
Photo by Barry Martyn

It's Halloween, and a distinctive pickup truck, easily recognizable by the barbecue hardware in the back, is parked on the corner of Dauphine and Lesseps,
deep in the Ninth Ward, just by Vaughan's Bar and Grill. Kermit's habit of spon-
taneously cooking up for anyone who feels hungry has brought hot sausage to
many people, and consternation to a few. A friend of mine from out of town once
looked through the windows of Café Brazil, saw what he thought was a car on
fire, and took off down Frenchmen before the gas tank blew.

Vaughan's is featuring Kermit Ruffins and his Barbecue Swingers, as it has
done most Thursday nights for a number of years. The band is Emile Vinet,
piano; Kevin Morris, bass; Corey Henry, trombone; and Shannon Powell, drums.
The musical menu is described by the leader as "traditional swing"—basically,
nice old songs from decades ago, played with equal amounts of sincerity and musicianship. It's an unlikely formula for commercial success in the current musical
climate of the city, but it certainly has worked for Kermit Ruffins. He's not the
most technically complex player—there are plenty of those in New Orleans—but
he has great stage presence and charisma. And a sense of fun. Tonight being Halloween, Kermit has come as a convict, in a white shirt and trousers with broad
black horizontal stripes. The penitentiary effect is alleviated by his boisterous
geniality and fedora hat.

The atmosphere inside the bar is the usual New Orleans combination of soul
and sleaze, and the fifty or so habitués in the place obviously like it that way. Behind

the bar, the usual lady is dressed as a fairy, with netting wings and a black tutu. Each beer is delivered with a few dance steps and a kind of fairy flutter, although the pliés might have been more elegant without the black Doc Marten boots.

The music is advertised for 10:00 P.M., so promptly at 11:20 the band kicks off with "Please Don't Talk about Me." It's the kind of music that welcomes people in, straightforward and warmhearted and unquestionably in the New Orleans tradition. Kermit has identified a niche for himself, that of Louis Armstrong–type trumpet-playing singer/entertainer—like a latter-day black Louis Prima. A party of bearded gentlemen revelers wearing wigs, false bosoms, and fishnet tights comes in as the band launches into "Tiger Rag." First in the solo order is trombonist Corey Henry, who tears off four immaculate choruses before wandering off for a beer. He's wearing white gloves, a full-length red robe with white trim, and a large golden crown studded with imitation jewelry.

Trumpet players Gregg Stafford and James Andrews arrive within minutes of each other, just as the band winds up "World on a String" to close the set. Kermit picks up the mike: "And now, y'all, we gonna take a reefer break—OH NO! Why did I say that? I made a mistake." The band files through the fire exit in the corner behind the drum kit to chill out on the Dauphine Street sidewalk. It's really not the time or place for any kind of interview, but we do manage a few minutes' chat.

Kermit's playing career began with a ten-year stint fronting the Rebirth Brass Band, which ended in 1993. He combined his interest in older styles of jazz (sparked by sitting in at the Palm Court Café) with his extrovert presentational style to form the Barbecue Swingers. He has the ability to deliver old-time hip nonsense with complete sincerity: "We gonna bring you back to one of those good old tunes, so flip your fedoras, and swing out like the rest of us!"

The band started with a Monday night residency at the Little People's Place, a bar in the Tremé owned by Kermit's in-laws. At the time, Kermit had no thought of wider success; he was just happy to have somewhere to play his favorite music. But a one-time appearance at Jazz Fest led to a recording contract with Justice Records. The band's first CD, *World on a String,* recorded at Ultrasonic Studios, got good reviews and did well.

He's confronted by the problem that faces all bands that win approval in the wider music scene: either spend long periods on the road to bring home lots of money, or stay home and maximize on the opportunities New Orleans can offer. Musicians from the city get homesick when they're out for a long time and are apt to spend a fortune on foreign pay phones, just to catch up on neighborhood gossip. (When Fats Domino was due to tour at the height of his career, he used

"Don't plead pity, feed that kitty": Kermit Ruffins, Jackson Square, 1992

Photo by Peter Nissen

to disappear to try to avoid leaving the city. Dave Bartholomew would have to threaten legal action to get him onto the tour bus.)

Kermit muses,

Life's so short, it's not a rehearsal, you know? Ten years with the Rebirth, eight years at Vaughan's—time's going by, all the time. Sure, I have to leave New Orleans sometimes—selling records and making money is real important, but to me it's just as important to be home, where my roots are. Even before I had the family, when I didn't really know what I was missing, I always liked to be able to just go home. It would be a lot easier if I could take the family with me when I go on the road, like the real big-timers do. But you know how long it takes to get into that league.

There's just something about being in your own place. If some manager told me I had to move away from home to find a wider market, I'd probably end my career right there—I could never leave New Orleans. I'd be up there in New York or somewhere, crying my eyes out in some hotel room, when I could be hanging out in the Tremé, laughing my ass off. Don't get me wrong, I like money, but I just need enough to cover the bare necessities that makes me happy, and it doesn't take much. More than that, and I'm overexcited.

Back inside Vaughan's, as I listen to the band roaring through "Skokiaan" and munch a dish of the red beans and rice that comes with the cover charge, it occurs to me how enviable Kermit is. He has what he wants, and wants what he has.

A Note on the Tambourine and Fan Club

As Milton Batiste, a trumpeter with Dejan's Olympia Brass Band, explained in the mid-eighties,

> The Tambourine and Fan was a club formed in conjunction with the New Orleans Recreation Department, to entertain the kids, and to teach them about dance, our culture, our heritage and to keep them off the streets, against drugs and other criminal activities.
>
> There is a place in the seventh ward on Claiborne Avenue where the club house is situated on city property, under the overpass. There were Mardi Gras Indians, there were dance teams, and there were sports—football, baseball and basketball.

Milton Batiste, 1993 *Photo by Mike Peters*

In it were a few musicians, young boys playing instruments. Freddy Kohlman and a couple of older musicians had at one time been helping these young musicians to learn to play. They had a band; they called it Tambourine and Fan Brass Band. It was getting nowhere. I stepped into the picture and said to the director, Jerome Smith, "I'd like to come in and tutor these guys and show 'em how to play the tunes and help out." We had summer camp, every summer with these kids, and I would go maybe twice a week to the fieldhouse and sorta try to shape them into what would become a band.[30]

The band Milton took over became the Junior Olympia band, but there had been other people besides Freddy Kohlman helping at the fieldhouse. Danny Barker had formed the Roots of Jazz Brass Band a couple of years earlier, and immediately before that, the Tambourine and Fan Club had spawned the Young Men Brass Band.

The musicians from these bands turned into quite a catalog of talent. There were Stafford Agee, trombone (Junior Olympia, regular Olympia, Rebirth); Revert Andrews, trombone (Junior Olympia, All Stars, Dirty Dozen); Keith Anderson, trombone and bass horn (Regal, Rebirth, Dirty Dozen, Olympia); Tanio Hingle and Kerry Hunter, drums (Junior Olympia, regular Olympia, New Birth); and Kenneth Terry (Junior and regular Olympia, Regal, Rebirth, Tremé) among others.

In a very real sense, the clubhouse under the overpass produced a vital contribution to the ongoing New Orleans brass band scene.

It was this aspect of Tambourine and Fan that I had originally intended to discuss when I made the appointment with its director, Jerome Smith. But we digressed, and I'm really glad we did.

Jerome Smith, Community Leader

Moving force behind the Tambourine and Fan Club

Interviewed at the Tremé Community Center, St. Philip and Villere Streets,

October 2002

Tremé Community Center,
St. Philip and Villere

Photo by Barry Martyn

*Tambourine and Fan is really an extension of the Mississippi Freedom Schools, a back-
drop from the civil rights movement. I was involved in much of that, the freedom riders
and the sit-ins and the jails and all those activities. There was always, when I was a
young boy, music at the school across the street [Craig School] before this community was
ruptured, one, by the Armstrong Park, and two, by the I-10 expressway. The expressway
took and ruptured the rhythms of the neighborhood. For example, when I was a boy in
the neighborhood . . . see this box? Without anyone telling a kid—these things happen as
if by osmosis—most of the youngsters started playing on boxes and bottles, etc., etc.*

*Now, if a band was to come through the neighborhood, at times, a few of us would
jump out of the windows of Craig School to follow the procession. Where this building
stands, you had the great Batiste family, right across the street from the school. So that
meant, with that family, you had music right there. That family is the root of the original Dirty Dozen, the kazoo band. So all that was happening on this block.*

*What happened, when those trees was taken down [on Claiborne], that was a gath-
ering place—it was an extension of every house in the neighborhood, for all kinds of
celebration and participation and rites of passage. Where the I-10 came through, a lot of
families had to move out. So that affected the observation and participation and total acceptance of the musical inheritance. In this area at one time or another, on every block,
somebody could play something. So that was a serious intrusion. And all that affects the*

mentality of folks. On occasions of joy and sorrow, you do not have that groundswell of participation that you once had. That's a serious negative.

I think it was basically racist, 'cause people were helpless. I mean we did not know that was going to happen. It was like, you would go to sleep at night, and when you wake up the next morning, the trees are gone, that kind of thing. Because there was an absence of power on this side, this black side, this neighborhood. Plus no respect for it. There's a lot of hypocrisy in terms of loving the music that was popularized by Louis Armstrong, but they destroy the ingredients that made Armstrong—see, that's so crucial.

One of the things that happens now, young people don't have—it's something more important than a musical instrument—is the vision and the sound. Because if you don't have that vision, and you don't have that sound, the instrument's not going to happen. The kids are not going to pick up the boxes, they're not going to pick up the bottles. That vision, and that sound, drives you towards trying to copy what you see with those men on the instruments. But you have to have the rituals of community for this kind of music. Once the rituals are threatened, then it affects the music.

It's affected in many ways, even today. There's a certain kind of dignity that's dictated by occasion and moment—but once this linkage is broken, the kids lose the lessons of being appropriate to the moment. At funerals and even, in many ways, the social gatherings—what they call the second lines, from the marching clubs—there was always certain protocols ingrained by being a witness to them, as opposed to having a written script. We know the limits and the inner dynamics of certain things. We knew the placement, as it related to person and participation.

What kept the old order stable wasn't just having jobs but having each other. You had each other before a job came into being. The sense of having each other—one thing about the city being called the Big Easy: it was almost impossible, in the time I'm talking about, for anyone to go hungry.

You had an extension of family that was beyond your physical dwelling, and the music is more powerful than your economic placement. We are not talking about the music in terms of the day of the funeral, or the day of a second line. The music here was daily, and all day. One thing I had enjoyed when I first went to New York: I stayed up on 110th Street, and when we came out in the morning, I heard all these drums; late that night, they were still playing. It reminded me of the way you hear things in bits and pieces on the blocks in the area here.

Now, the music, the sound, to me, indicated a kind of personal linkage. No one was complaining about the sound. As opposed to the intrusions in this neighborhood—folks are complaining about the music at night, because it disturbs them. Now, when I was a young man, there was no disturbance. Music could go on all day, all night, because it was ingrained into the spirit of the people. So folks leave, and intruders come in and have no sense of what we loosely call the "culture," but what is greater than the word "culture," it was about a life existence where the music and the people were one and the same.

When I was a boy, we had a full-time music teacher, years ago, across the street at Craig School. We don't have a full-time music teacher now—may get it once or twice a week. That's not good enough. That's a disrespect for the heritage, that's a serious disrespect. It's almost vulgar, not to have a full-time music instructor across the street from a park that's named after Louis Armstrong. It's sinful.

Until it's time to do showcasings—cutting down on the educational budget, you can relate that to the White House—they say they don't want to leave no child behind. But there's no universal guarantee on class sizes, there's no universal guarantee on music in the schools, there's no universal guarantee on improving teachers' pay. So there's something in the White House that's dangerous to the total existence of elevating people to the levels of certain kinds of equality. And that's right across the country. The other thing is it was clearly at a time in history when, on the black side, you were locked out in a more rigid sense. It forced you inward to find a kind of comfort that enables you to make the day.

For example, even in the funeral processions, older musicians can lay on a note with a certain kind of spiritual grace that younger musicians are not able to achieve. They're conditioned by another kind of circumstance. They tend to have, in some strange way, a disconnect—it makes them rush towards giving a kind of emotional nourishment coming out of that horn. And that destroys the majestic feeling. As Harold Dejan said, "Have patience. You have to bring yourself to it." And Danny Barker said, "Don't rush it." And that grace would come from that restraint.

The dancing changed because it's conditioned by another kind of social approach; there's been a rupture of the protocols. For example, some young people who were exposed to the Olympia band—Tanio Hingle and a few others that came off Hunter's Field Tambourine and Fan—they were exposed to Batiste and Mr. Dejan. Once they got into a thing with the older musicians, they can enter that, because they had a direction; they bring their person to it in a different way.

But there's been a breakdown in terms of the music and the church. The generation of Mr. Dejan, and others, when they play the hymns and the dirges and that kind of thing, the instrument is only an extension of the voice, which is about their participation in that environment, where the processions were an extension of what came out of the church, that dictated a certain dignity that was accepted by whoever.

Now, because youngsters are not church based, in terms of dealing with the rituals, that makes for a certain kind of emotional projection. So the dance has changed—it hasn't lost the energy but a certain kind of grace and dignity.

It's a definite: change will be. But I don't think there's been any change in the breeding of people; there's no change there. Within the music, when the disconnect becomes serious enough, it will not be able to be defined in terms of how it was created originally. And that would definitely bring about a loss.

I seriously think that the music and the culture are going to split, because one of the things that's troubling: there was music for the sake of the music, for the sake of the spirit. There is now a kind of thing that's like the American presence coming into the village, and then commercialization can affect what was hidden, what was protected by separation from that.

There is an absence of the broad-based spiritual connection, and certain feelings cannot enter the music. There's a broader-based breakdown of community rituals, too. This ability, in New Orleans, of saying, "Good morning" and "Good evening," as simple as that is—that loss speaks of a kind of devaluing of a collective dignity. Because what that says is that I care about you, and you care about me—for me to recognize your presence and your humanity. That's been lost, and that will definitely affect the creative process. If that's not a part of the music, that recognition of universal humanity, then we lose that; we don't carry it over to everything we do.

That's when we hit a nonsound, that's not human, in my estimation. You cannot disregard the human presence and then say you're going to do something that's going to express a totality of that. One reason why, whether it was Red Allen or Louis Armstrong or Mr. Dejan—I mean when Harold said, "Everything is lovely"—that's not secular, that's a spiritual thing. When we had the Tambourine and Fan, Milton Batiste would always come around. He had a dominant presence that attracted kids like a kind of Santa Claus. On the streets, with that horn, his presence, his whole style was a major attraction.

One of the key things—I'll be writing a note to the folks in the city and in the school systems—is that it's important that they cultivate the audience for the music. Musicians gonna come, one way or another, but it's important that the music be played. Like with the Armstrong centenary—you have all these big celebrations, the this, the that, the airport—the sin is, you don't have the music and the children's ear: that will reach their heart. Except for youngsters who are around musicians and round Tambourine and Fan, but just generally. That's because they don't play it. The key is that, with the neighborhood breaking down, it needs to be played in the schools. Not as a lesson or a classroom assignment: it has to become part of the fabric. A daily thing: when you come in on certain days, you play Armstrong. Other times, it's the Olympia band. The music would become a part of the children's daily lives. You cultivate the audience, and they're going to make the appeal for the music. They have to know that the music is of them, and from them.

There's a lot of social and pleasure clubs, but that's not really a good measuring stick;

I think the activities that don't exist in the neighborhoods is a better measure. You don't have unorganized consistent music activities that was popularized by a certain kind of lifestyle, where bands would come through if it was a prize fight—in the back of the yards for neighborhood suppers, bands would just come in, and folks would be just playing on the porches and stuff. Now this is not professional activities, and the folks would come and sit in. Most of what you see now is organized activities—that's a little different.

With the Batiste family here, any day or night somebody might start beating on a garbage can; a line would form up and go round the block, just for the goodness of doing it. We had a high school not too far from here, Clark High School. They turned out some great musicians that came from around here—one was James Black—oodles of musicians that was top of the heap. Most of the them was exposed to that concept of the music being locked into the block, locked into the house. That's gone.

For example, we used to be coming down the street, going to school, say from first grade up until high school, and you would hear them singing the different sounds on the street. "I got rags, I got rags. . . ." And the cowbell ringing. And on another corner, "Watermelon, red to the rind. . . . Tomatoes, bananas." You go up two blocks later, different time of day, I'm talking about serious tap dancers—lyrical dancers. All this is right in the neighborhood, just saturated with it.

When the society was tight, segregation was rigid, rigid, rigid. We needed to invent things to maintain sanity, beyond commercialization. Now that's not needed, to deal with sanity. The music is driven by a desire to make money. Originally, it was based on a need to survive—the money came into that too, because you could make money dancing and singing, and you could eat. But there was also this other thing, like it was also done just for the goodness of doing it. The people—not the professional musicians—the presence of the music in their lives, as Joe Blow, playing the drums, playing the saxophone for the joy of it, this gave the music a foundation.

One of the dangers of the civil rights thing was there was this great desire to assimilate, into the unknown, and we lost something in the transfer. When we had segregated schools, we had full-time music people. Years after so-called integration, there's no full-time music teaching—this situation has existed for years. What I'm saying is there is a negative in terms of the way people relate to themselves. In terms of broad-based racism, in terms of certain kinds of personal dignity, the civil rights movement did that.

But there's some other things that were lost—looking at ourselves through someone else's eyes, where we would open up to our own spirit and maintain the rituals that enabled us to cross the bridge, the rituals of faith that enabled us to survive the indignities, to fight against them. Once we thought we had a clearance zone, we separated ourselves from certain things. And that indeed was a loss. In this community, where you would

JEROME SMITH, COMMUNITY LEADER　129

be slapped in the mouth for not saying "Good morning" or "Good evening," where you would be punished for passing your neighbor's garbage can and not taking it out of the gutter and putting it by the step, those things were all wrapped into the artistic expressions, too. We see that in many ways. Some of those things we are trying to reestablish, having young people not only to look at what's being generated by their day but spend time trying to discover more about the men of the music and how they entered the music.

My position is—as long as babies are being born, and there's not universal abortion—it's our obligation to flash the light. If you try not to see the day through your eyes—because sophistication sometimes brings about a blindness—see it through a kid's eyes. If you can find some way to enter that, you can be a force of guidance, backwards and forwards, understanding that at some point, you have to back off and trust the experience that you shared with them.

We had a thing where some youngsters wanted me to go and listen at a rap thing some of them were doing. So we struck this bargain. I said, "Well, look. I'll go to this if you go hear Miles." Miles Davis was coming in to do the Jazz Fest.

And so they went to hear Miles. And a youngster came out of the concert, and he said, "You know what Miles reminds me of?" I said, "No, what?" He said, "Miles reminds me of a Mardi Gras Indian." Miles has a habit of bringing the musicians to him and sending them away again—which is the exact same thing as a Mardi Gras Indian does. I didn't see that, the kid did. And then the kid says, "But the other thing is, Miles mixes it up." Another kid said, "Miles sounds like a flower." This is a youngster around five or six.

The greatest moment I ever had was with Louis Armstrong in 1949 when he was by the old Caldonia—he was on a float for the Zulus, and there was all these elderly people coming. This was like Mardi Gras day. They were so excited—until the day was no longer Mardi Gras—they were so excited, they were crying. And it wasn't about Zulu, it wasn't about Mardi Gras, it wasn't about none of that—for some of those people, they were old enough to remember Louis as a child. And that's what I witnessed, right on that corner. They were just locked into him. I thank God I was able to witness that. Some of them couldn't believe it. It was as though it wasn't Louis Armstrong the great world musician; it was more like Louis Armstrong who was walking the streets, playing in the neighborhood round here—it was that Louis Armstrong. It was like they knew something about him that the world did not know, that was special to them. That was a moment. I'm telling you.

With young people and the music—if they get close to essentials, they bring something forward, if they get close to a linkage.

With the absence of Milton Batiste, Harold Dejan, and Danny Barker, Lionel Batiste Sr. is the link. Not just in terms of his instrument, but he's the last of the old-time *stylists. You can have him, and these younger drummers, like Tanio Hingle and Keith Frazier, and this one and that one—if Uncle Lionel is there, the kids that's five, six, seven, they're going to listen to Uncle Lionel. There's something about the way he plays.*

Back in 1970, we all danced off the bass drum. But that's not so now. With Tanio, Fatman [Kerry Hunter], James Andrews, some of the younger cats, they can enter that old thing, and the bass drum gives you recovery times.

Even with all the things we spoke of, there's a uniqueness of expression about music in New Orleans, and a feeling that it's not all over.

New Birth Brass Band
Majestic Brass Band
Algiers Brass Band
All Star Brass Band
Regal Brass Band
Tremé Brass Band
Doc Paulin Brass Band
Pinstripe Brass Band
New Wave Brass Band
Mahogany Brass Band

Cayetano "Tanio" Hingle, Bass Drum

BORN: New Orleans, November 14, 1969

Began at Tambourine and Fan with the Bucket Men Brass Band, which became the Junior
Olympia; now plays with the Olympia Brass Band and leads the New Birth Brass Band

Interviewed at 3621 Burgundy Street, November 2002

*My name is Cayetano Miller Hingle—they call me
Tanio. My name is Spanish. I was in Spain with
Milton Batiste and the Olympia Band and there
was a street called "Cayetano."*

*I started out with the Tambourine and Fan
band on Hunter's Field. They had a lot of organized athletics. I had attended the elementary
school that Tambourine and Fan was associated
with; they had their own social and pleasure club.
That's when Danny Barker came over to the club
on Hunter's Field and started a band called the
Roots of Jazz. That was in 1983.*

*I picked up drums from listening to Leroy
Breaux and Lionel Batiste. Mr. Milford Dolliole gave me my first drum. He
lived exactly across the street from the school I was going to. We would see Duke
Dejan picking Mr. Dolliole up to work with the Olympia Brass Band. I was still
playing ball out there with the youth, but when we went to get dressed, we could
hear the band practicing. Danny was teaching all those young cats how to play.*

*At Tambourine and Fan, we started a little band—we were just going around playing
with boxes and stuff. The guy who was over Tambourine and Fan, Jerome Smith, he went
to Milton Batiste and asked if he would come and help the kids. I knew about the old
tradition, by me being at a lot of old jazz funerals. My daddy was part of a social and
pleasure club, the Sixth Ward High Steppers. That was one of the original clubs that first
came out. And there was the Sixth Ward High Rollers, and the Sixth Ward Diamonds,
and the Old Money Wasters, the Old Caldonia. I was just out there watching the parades,
and the bands coming down the street. The feeling I used to catch when we were there
was just like, wow! It was a joyful feeling at all times.*

*I started playing bass drum in the band they had at my elementary school, at the
age of eight. Straight march music, but the first song we learned was "The Saints." We*

135

played it off the music, but by the time sixth grade came, a couple of guys in the neighbor-
hood was in a band, and they was from Tambourine and Fan. We heard the music on the
Hunter's Field at the same time, so we took it on our own to start a little jazz band.

At first, the name of the band was the Bucket Men Brass Band. There was me, Staf-
ford Agee, Abraham Cosse, Kenneth Terry, Kerry Hunter. Jerome Smith's son, Taju, he
was a bass drummer also; we played together. A couple of years later—we were still with
Milton [Batiste]—Mr. Dejan came out. He said, "Hey, Bat! You keep holding them
boys in the shade—when are they going on a gig?" So Bat said, "Would you want them
on a gig?" Duke said, "They know 'Lord, Lord, Lord!' They're ready." So after that the
Olympia had a gig one night; Milton told us to put on our red jackets, black pants, white
shirts. We went to the gig, and next day, Harold said, "That's the Junior Olympia." Mil-
ton said, "You know what? That's a good name." They named it right then and there.

When we were coming up, we had to be at Milton's house every Tuesday at five
o'clock to practice—we learned "Lord, Lord, Lord," "Just a Little While," and so forth.
For the traditional songs, we were working out of the Fake Book. That was at the begin-
ning, but after about two weeks, the book had to go.

Erskine Campbell played the clarinet and saxophone. A couple of weeks later, Revert
Andrews and Glen Andrews came in; they're first cousins, their mothers are sisters. I
tried to keep the traditional beat on bass drum; I like that groove.

In the last eight years, I changed a little bit. Now I play with and lead the New Birth
Brass Band. Some of the music we play is contemporary, but we play more traditional
music than any of the other younger brass bands—we learned from tradition, playing
under Milton Batiste. The New Birth was formed in 1987, from part of the All Stars and
part of the Junior Olympia. Our tuba player, Kerwin James, was with the All Stars, but he
was also the backup tuba player with the Junior Olympia. His brother Philip Frazier is
the leader of the Rebirth Brass Band.

When we started, it was a French Quarter thing. At that time, we didn't want gigs.
We were making more money playing on the street. We'd set up in the Quarter around ten
o'clock in the morning, get finished at seven in the evening, and that's that. We played
on Jackson Square—Tuba was on one side, we were on the other. Half an hour each, that
was us. There was a regular seven people in the band. Sometimes, we'd go out with eight.

The Olympia Brass Band's bass drummer, [Nowell] "Pa Pa" Glass, was a good
person to follow behind and to play music behind. A couple of summers ago, I went to
Spain with the Olympia: me, Pa Pa, Boogie and Kerry, Jeffrey Hills, and Edgar Smith on
tubas—so there were two bass drummers, two snare drummers and two tuba players—it
was a big show. Milton let the people know; the old guys would get off the stage and let

the young ones do the gig! That's what we did. We all played together for forty minutes, and then he left us alone for the last twenty.

Milton was trying to let the people know that there was a lot of younger cats gonna be coming. It had showed them that we could play the traditional things, by us playing with the big band. But for the last twenty minutes, he would tell the audience, "We're going to let the younger guys do what they do, to let y'all know where the music is going right now in New Orleans." Sometimes we would fool Milton—on some of the funky music, we would play the traditional beat.

The way I do it with the Olympia, that's how I was taught to do it in the beginning, with the straight traditional beat, and keeping the New Orleans feeling. There's a lot of beats that you can play, but if you ain't got that New Orleans groove, to me there's no more brass band. Sometimes, I get away from it. I'm sorry we have to get away from it, but it's the change in times and the music and sometimes the crowd that we're performing for.

I had to straighten a couple of people out a couple of weeks ago about funk. I said, "Y'all say we're playing funk. But if that's the case, we could take 'Just a Little While to Stay Here' and funk it up. I would come in with a different beat. If I take a Herbie Hancock song like 'Chameleon' and play it with a funky beat, it's gonna sound funky. But I could just as easily play it with a traditional beat."

The Tremé Brass Band, with Benny Jones and Lionel, they ain't leaving a pocket. You can tell them to play anything in the world. I love the way the old cats played, like Lionel Batiste and Stanley Stephens. A lot of people say to me that I must have been around a long time. I've been listening and watching and looking at these cats and say- ing, "Man, that's real New Orleans." Ever since the day I picked up that drum and started playing that beat, I never looked back. This is my life.

The New Birth works three or four times a week. For wedding receptions, conventions, press parties. We're going out to Brazil on November 6. We play a parade every year in Philadelphia. The club scene ain't happening too much right now.

At one time, we were the house band at Donna's Bar and Grill. That would have been around 1996. We did it once or twice a week for about five years, on a Wednesday and Saturday. Then, before you know it, we started doing Wednesday, Friday, and Sun- day. It was working out. You couldn't retire on the money, but it was good exposure, and it gave us a chance to sell CDs. We got more gigs from it, because a lot of people would hire us to work in Europe and different parts of the U.S. by seeing us at Donna's.

There ain't no "Today, I'm gonna do my garden. I ain't gonna talk about music, I ain't gonna play my horn, I ain't gonna play my drum." I used to go by Milton's house every single day. That telephone, and that studio—something happening at all times!

CAYETANO "TANIO" HINGLE, BASS DRUM 137

With this music business, you can't sit home and wait—it's not happening. Milton is the one that was the teacher about going to get it.

I lived in the Seventh Ward, right between Esplanade and St. Bernard. When I was younger, I hung in the Tremé twenty-four hours a day—that's where all the culture's at. Congo Square, the Caldonia, Dirty Dozen Brass Band, Chosen Few Brass Band, Kermit Ruffins, Lil' Rascals Brass Band, Tremé Brass Band, Pinstripes, Coolbone, Soul Rebels, everybody—they all hang out, before they go to the gig. Stop at Joe's Cozy Corner, get them a cold one, load up the cars, get to the gig. Meet at Joe's two hours before, get to the job forty-five minutes before the start, everything gonna be all right.

We have a big following. We work about every other Sunday on parades in the season. They have different clubs coming out now and younger bands coming up. They don't worry me; I like to play with them too. A lot of them are playing the right kind of music. Not too many of them are playing traditional—that's what we're missing right now.

The modern stuff that the young bands play now, it comes from their heart—it's their own feeling. Three or four guys sitting in a room, humming, patting their feet—the stuff they're coming out with is out of their own heads. They get on their horns and play what they been humming—could be just some phrase like "Your head too big"—"Ba bom bom Bom." A lot of stuff starts like that.

Kenneth "Little Milton" Terry, Trumpet

BORN: New Orleans, 1969

Played with the Bucket Men Brass Band, the Junior Olympia Brass Band, the New Birth Brass Band, the Rebirth Brass Band, the Chosen Few Brass Band, the Tremé Brass Band, and the Regal Brass Band

Interviewed at his home on Urquhart Street, October 2002

Actually, years ago, it was kind of funny how I came to music. Growing up in New Orleans, you always see like a funeral or parade. I'd see a guy playing a horn, people dancing, and I was inspired by that. I started playing cornet at school, in the fifth grade. I wanted to give playing the second lines a shot, so me and some of the guys, we were all playing sports together, got together and started to teach ourselves to pick out the notes— no formal teaching for that. This was in the neighborhood around Urquhart Street, just outside the Tremé. We just started walking round the street, trying to play.

I was playing sports over at Tambourine and Fan, and the coach had seen us playing music. So they brought us into the Tambourine and Fan, and we just sat in a room and started practicing. We were the first band they had, and we were called the Bucket Men Brass Band. That came about because Tambourine and Fan had a second line club called the Bucket Men.

Through time, around six or seven months later, we were introduced to Milton Batiste. He used to sit us down in the locker room by the field, and we'd just try to learn to play the songs. He always used to holler at me, "Boy, you're playing the wrong note." At first, it was intimidating, because here's a guy that you see all over the city, playing music, and I'm there trying to learn from him. So he tells me I was playing the wrong note, I got kind of nervous, fussing that the next note might be wrong too. But he just kept at it. I used to think, "Shit, I don't know if I should be doing this." He always said, "Kenneth, you gotta make the note." The first song he taught me was "Down by the Riverside." I still remember that.

After that we carried on practicing by Tambourine and Fan, twice a week, I think it was Tuesdays and Thursday. We would start around six or seven o'clock, and we were always the last to leave the organization—we were in the back, practicing our horns. Then we did a couple of gigs under the name of the Bucket Men Brass Band. We had Stafford Agee, Taju Smith (Revert Andrews came later), Abraham Cosse when we finally got a tuba player, Kerry Hunter on snare, Tanio Hingle on bass drum. There was a guy we called "Specs"; his right name was David Gallaud. We had about ten or twelve young guys.

Then we started practicing at someone's house, so the band got smaller. There was me, Revert Andrews on trombone, Glen Andrews on trumpet, Tanio and Kerry, Abraham Cosse, and Erskine Campbell (Kid Merv's brother) on saxophone. That was when it became the Junior Olympia.

How it happened, Milton Batiste had a gig somewhere, and we used to always go with him to listen. So he said, "Man, what y'all think about changing the name of the band?" And he talked to us about keeping the tradition going, for the sake of the music. He was always telling us not to ever leave the tradition. Then he suggested using the name Junior Olympia. The guys were real excited: here's the number one band in the city of New Orleans asking us to be the junior band! So we said, "Yeah, why not?"

That was around 1982. We used to go by his house and rehearse. We had like a real closed rehearsal—we didn't allow too many people to come in. We had to concentrate on what we were doing—we were there for one reason, to learn. We'd sit in the practice room and listen to old recordings by Louis Armstrong, the Olympia, the Young Tuxedo. Then we'd try to play the tunes. Every rehearsal, before we left, we'd learn at least three traditionals. We knew the songs as a group, and we could play them the way we wanted to.

And we were listening to the Rebirth, the Dirty Dozen, and the Chosen Few. One day in the practice room we started playing "Tuba Fats." Milton went into a rage. He told us, "Don't you ever come back here playing that shit! Whatever you do, I want you to stick to the tradition. See all that other stuff? It's no good." Believe it or not, to this day, the traditional music is still what's happening.

I've been in the Bucket Men, the Junior Olympia, the Jackson Square Brass Band, the Original New Birth (I was there before James Andrews—he was still with the All Stars), the Rebirth, the Chosen Few, the Tremé, the Regal, and I get gigs with bands all over the city—the Algiers, the Pinstripe—I worked with just about everybody, and now I'm getting gigs at Preservation Hall. And that's all because of one thing—sticking with the tradition.

A couple of years later, the Junior Olympia branched off. We were going playing in the Quarter; Milton didn't like that. We'd say to him, "We're not practicing today; we're going to play in the French Quarter." He'd say, "What? You come and practice!" He and his wife used to come to pick us up to practice, and we used to have to run from them. It was like, go make a few dollars, or go practice. He got fed up with us. He got to the point of thinking, "Oh shit, they're going out there—just let them go." We went out there, and we wound up missing a gig. It was a benefit. We were young; we thought, "Why go play for free, when we can make some money?"

Milton was highly upset, and we fell out for a couple of years. We had a couple of guys leaving, and the All Stars was breaking up. So we welded together and formed the

New Birth. The All Stars and the Junior Olympia both knew a lot of traditional stuff,
and we started to combine that with the sort of thing the Rebirth was doing, so we had it
all. We used to go playing in Jackson Square with Stackman [Elliott Callier]—he used to
teach us stuff. One day, Benny Jones came out. He said to me, "Hey, Little Milton, you
want to make a gig?" I told him I had to ask my momma.

I was about fourteen. Benny and Tuba brought me home in the back of a truck to my
home at 1220 Franklin Avenue to ask if I could go. After that, I started working with the
Chosen Few.

Then, when Benny started his Tremé band, he had me and Kermit Ruffins on trum-
pet. They called me "Little Milton" or "Little Half Head" because I had been Milton's
protégé. I know I was very influenced by his style, and now when I play at the Hall on
Sunday nights, I'm actually taking his spot. That's a huge step, going right behind some-
one like that who was in that spot for years. Jacques Gauthé, the soprano player, always
shouts, "Play it, Milton," when I take a solo.

At first, they said I looked like Milton because I was a bandleader; I played trumpet
and tambourine. Later on, when I started getting a stomach, I really looked like him.

In 1989, I went to Ascona [festival in Switzerland] for the first time with Benny Jones
and the Tremé. Ascona was a good experience at one time, and then it kind of went down.

I joined the Rebirth much later on, in the nineties. I had been with the New Birth,
and Kermit had left the Rebirth. They took Glen Andrews and me. I was there for a
while—it was a good experience. When I was in the band, they had Roddy Paulin on
saxophone—he used to write a lot of stuff we would read off the paper, but a lot of the
stuff they do is by ear.

It was a different thing from a normal brass band. Sometimes we would pick up on
things kids would be saying on the street—we'd put a melody to it, and before you knew
it, it's a song. We'd just do it on the spot. Sometimes, we'd play one riff for the whole of a
four-hour parade. Towards the end, it would be a song.

I had trained by playing chord changes, and I found switching to a one-chord-based
funk thing more difficult than I thought. In the New Birth, now, we play some things that
have no chord changes at all, just a straight line. Then I go to Preservation Hall, and I
have to play all the chord changes. You have to be versatile. Actually, what happened to
me on Wednesday, I was sitting up there playing traditional things, and I had been used to
playing straight lines. I mean, I knew the songs, but by the time I had moved to the chord,
they had all changed to another one. I find playing on chords easier, it makes you think.
With the other thing, they put down a bass line, and you can run with that all day. At the
Hall, it's fine. You get to play with some of them old guys and play the old things. I don't
have no complaints. It's a learning experience, and the more you learn, the better it is.

KENNETH "LITTLE MILTON" TERRY, TRUMPET 141

If you look at it, they got a lot of kids trying to play this music, and they don't know anything about traditional songs or anything. Tuba's still calling me to go to Jackson Square and pick up those old songs. Kermit used to sit over by Tuba and say, "Tuba, everything you play, I'm, going to steal it."

But it's real hard to play in what we call a "street" brass band and then go and play in one of those jazz clubs. I like to do both, like with the New Birth.

At one time, there were only a few social and pleasure clubs, but now there are many of them. They like the street brass—something about playing from the soul, the heart. Also, there are some clubs that don't want anything but traditional music, even some of the younger clubs.

The music changes just like the seasons of the year. I can stay up with it, no problem. But it's still hard to make the switch. It takes time to make the adjustment—the feeling is totally different. I mean you try and play a straight line with those chords behind you, you're going to be stuck.

When I was coming up, I used to listen to a lot of Louis Armstrong on records—still do—but never tried to copy him. I know some on-the-way famous people right now that copy Louis note for note, but I never did that, that's not me. You don't have to: there's enough out there to give you plenty of inspiration.

Edgar "Sarge" Smith, Bass Horn

BORN: New Orleans, February 23, 1948

Played with Doc Paulin, co-led the Majestic Brass Band with Flo Anckle, played with Dejan's Olympia Brass Band for eighteen years; currently with Andrew Hall's Society Brass Band

Interviewed at 3621 Burgundy Street, October 2002

Before crack became an epidemic in New Orleans, we had the opportunity to see what it could do in New York City. It was like "When this gets to New Orleans, it's gonna fuck some shit up." Lo and behold.

—KEITH FRAZIER

And some of those smart kids who think you have to be completely knocked out to be a good hornman are just plain crazy. It isn't true. I know, believe me.

—CHARLIE PARKER,
Hear Me Talkin' to Ya

Purely from the music standpoint, the Olympia Brass Band was the crossover. It was the fork in the road, especially after Milton Batiste and Ernest ["Doc"] Wat-son and Boogie Breaux got in the band. Milton Batiste had played rhythm and blues, and so had Boogie and Doc Watson. When you get guys like that, who have a different insight into music, then you're gonna have that change. They still feel compassion for the old standards and the traditional music, but they want to add a little spice to the gumbo. That's the whole New Orleans thing: what you add to the gumbo. It opened up a lot of different avenues.

I was working with the Majestic Brass Band led by Himas Floyd Anckle, better known as "Flo." He had a bebop and rock 'n' roll background. He had worked with a lot of the big names; he played tenor and alto saxophones. He was a real good musi-cian, could read anything. Flo was a restless type of person. I had first met him when we worked together in Doc Paulin's band. We decided to leave that band and do our own thing. We wanted to try something else. We heard things like the Olympia playing "Hey Pocky Way." They were the first brass band to do it; they called it "Tuba Fats." Milton infused other things like "Hi Heel Sneakers."

Flo and I listened and thought we could do the same sort of thing. He was very much influenced by Louis Jordan, and he wanted to take that music to the street. We had Cyrille Salvant on cornet, Joe Taylor on bass drum, Lawrence Trotter on snare, Ayward Johnson on trombone, I was on trombone, and Tuba Fats was helping us out on bass horn. That's what inspired me to play sousaphone; up to then I had been playing trombone.

We started doing funerals, and a lot of people started to pay attention to us. That's how we got Jazz Fest in 1977. We got rave reviews. The only surviving members of that band besides me are Jerome Davis, Daryl Smith, Joe Taylor, and Daryl Walker. Then we got Joe Salisbury in the band on sax. The trend was getting the so-called genuine musicians—guys who could read, do parts, and play harmonies correctly. Later on, we had Greg Davis on trumpet for a while. We always had three trumpets playing three-part harmony. Two saxes and two trombones in harmony, bass horn, and two drummers.

Greg stayed with us a couple of years, and then he started the Dirty Dozen with Roger Lewis, who I think is one of the greatest reed men we have. He plays all reed instruments equally well, and you don't find that with a lot of musicians. He's dedicated himself to his craft—he's an excellent reader and an excellent orchestrator. He reads all the directions— if it says "pianissimo," you don't have to stop and say, "Wait, let's do that part softly."

I remember we were at Lawrence Trotter's house for a practice one Sunday, and Greg Davis told us, "I'm not going to be able to work with you so much. I'm starting my own band."

The Dirty Dozen started setting a different pace. They just picked it up—respected the traditional music but came up with their own thing. There's a lot of people who say they're not respecting the music, but I have to question their understanding.

The Dirty Dozen was number one for musicianship. The younger bands have the enthusiasm and fire, but they don't have the know-how. I'm not knocking, but I have to say, there are very few young brass bands that are paying their dues. Straight out of school, straight on the street. Guys say to me, "You still playing that old style." I tell them, "Well, it works. I'm playing what the tuba's supposed to play. Not trumpet or saxophone parts." I'm just glad that there's some younger musicians who are serious. Steve Johnson, the trombone player, comes to mind, and so do Jeffrey Hills on tuba, and Steve's brother, Ronell.

When the Dozen came on the street, they played a lot of cerebral music. Some of the younger musicians couldn't catch it, and they started using drugs. Get this right: I'm not saying that the Dirty Dozen encouraged drugs—they didn't. But some guys don't know how to separate realism from foolishness. That's the whole thing. I don't want to get into naming names, but we have some fantastic musicians who would be even greater if they only would stop using drugs, and I've had to counsel them. They come to my counseling office and talk to me; their wives come to my office and talk to me. They need help because of their addiction problem.

I've been doing that work for twenty-six years. The whole crack thing didn't come from the music. It was introduced into the schools by some criminally diseased minds to institute drugs in society. And the best way to make dope a staple in society is to put it in the schools. They pushed it in the school grounds to kids who were not mentally ready to face it. They had no concept of where tomorrow was going to come from. We're talking heroin, we're talking crystal meth, we're talking angel dust, things of this nature, sweeping through the schools like a plague.

The effect was devastating. A lot of musicians with time on their hands and money in their pockets found themselves at a point where they could experiment. So they'd buy a little angel dust. Start off by putting a little dust with some weed and smoke it. Then they start cooking up some heroin and smoking that, which is the worst way to be under that spell. It gets into your system faster.

I'm not going to sit here and tell you I'm Johnny Good—I've done a wide range of things myself in my time. One of them was smoking a bit of marijuana, but that gage makes me get fat—I can't afford that. I was the type of person that likes to be in control.

At one time, society seemed to treat drugs as a joke. You'd get comedians on stage making jokes about getting high and making jokes about seeing someone overdose. That kind of thing makes it acceptable, like, "If they can laugh about it, I can use it." Some of these guys I counsel say, "You like to eat. You're addicted too—you're just as bad." But the point is I'm not breaking into houses to go buy a poboy.

I ask people, "Do you realize where you are? See yourself: where do you expect to be? Before you answer, think about it. If you want help, I'm there for you day and night. But if you're just going to say things to placate me, I don't need it." I let them know the things I had to kick for myself. I didn't do a twelve-step program. The only thing I did was bend my knees and pray. In my case, I had a problem with alcohol. I loved my beer! Ricky Monie and I would go anywhere; he'd say to the bartender, "Give us two beers," and I'd say, "And give us two beers." It got worse.

Kicking any kind of addiction has to begin with the person: you have to make up your mind that you want to stop—you have to see what you can lose. As far as being a musician, you lose a lot of your patience, and then you lose a lot of your talent. Because, instead of worrying what comes out of the horn, you're worried about going out and getting some stuff and getting loaded. Then you start losing gigs, and you lose your credibility—if you keep on, you lose your soul. It's like working with a zombie. I don't profess to be any kind of goody-goody, but I know what it took for me, and I can only talk about that from my standpoint. It's a thing where you want to quit, and you need to quit.

The birth of my son was a big factor to me. We had to be two sober parents to bring up our child in a house full of love and sobriety. Nowadays, I may have a social glass of wine every three months.

I quit drinking in 1981, and that summer, I went to Europe with the Olympia. We went to Germany and finished up in Munich—you know that's where they have the best beer. Everybody in the band—including Watson—was saying, "Come on, Edgar, have a beer." They goaded me for three weeks. Oh man, that blond beer looked great in those big frosted steins. I just sat there. Everybody was having a joke; Harold was laughing, "Come on, cuz, have one with me." They knew what I was doing, and they were helping—they were testing me. I didn't understand; I would go back to my room, and I would be mad. I thought, "Mother fuckers, pulling that shit on me." Harold Dejan, being the gentleman he is, called me up a couple of days after we got home. He said, "Edgar, I'm proud of you. You know, we did that intentionally, to see just where your head was." He had got together with Milton and Watson and said, "Let's find out exactly where Edgar stands on this." There'll never be another Harold—no one will ever come close.

The drug problem in New Orleans isn't improving. The minute we get a handle on one problem, something else comes up. Now heroin is back—that's bad, bad, bad. You can get black tar heroin, white horse—all kinds of heroin, different versions of it. Once you think you've beat one villain, back comes an old enemy you thought you had subdued.

We have a program at my church called the "A Team." It's a group of ex–users who decided, with prayer and abstinence, that they would never do drugs again and would help others. You see a lot of churches doing this now, but ours was one of the first churches to come out against drugs and go out in the community. That's the Christian Unity Baptist Church, at 1700 Conti.

We don't have any federal sponsorship or city money; this program is purely generated by the church. We have a vast number of members, but we're not one of those mega churches that gets on TV, asking for money: you get preaching for two minutes, and asking for money for the other twenty-eight. We're a community church, made up of imperfect people—we listen to the perfect word. We don't have healing salve, we don't speak in tongues, we don't rock chandeliers, none of that crap. These faith healers are just shills—if you can cure people, why not take it to the hospitals?

Our church has had the Olympia Brass Band, the Tremé, and the Dirty Dozen. "Make a joyful noise unto the Lord."

Donna Poniatowski-Sims, Venue Proprietor

Interviewed at Donna's Bar and Grill, St. Ann and Rampart Streets, November 2002

Donna's Bar and Grill

Photo by Barry Martyn

I was born right here in New Orleans, so I grew up with an understanding of what the music is all about. I stayed here until I was five and then went away to school. It was at the age of eighteen that I came back, after I graduated. I always loved it—my first husband and I had a little place on Bourbon Street where a lot of musicians like the French brothers, George and Bob, used to come; that was back in 1977. The Olympia and all the older brass bands were around then, but not the younger ones.

The Tremé Brass Band didn't get going until about 1991—they were the first brass band we had in here. I knew about the brass band tradition, and I'd seen brass bands. But in the past the brass bands were rather limited to the jazz funerals, and that's one big difference between them and the younger bands.

My first husband had always planned to have a place like this. When we had the Bourbon Street place, we also had three very small children, so I couldn't put in the time. You know, when you run a small business, you have to put in more time than when you run a large business. We moved to Florida, and I was teaching there. But we always said that when we retired, we'd open a little jazz bar. So I stayed over there about two years, and then I decided to do what we had always said we would do together. I didn't have any real plans, but settled on this place. We started off kind of slow, as far as featuring the brass bands; I just played them largely on weekends.

Also, through me knowing Benny Jones, Kermit Ruffins started here on Monday nights. Then we added the Soul Rebels, because they had a new hip-hop brass band sound; there was a market for that. I told my husband Charlie, "If we stick to New Orleans music, we'll never be big, but we'll have our niche." We also had the New Birth, and the Pinstripe played in here for about three years. Then the leader of Pinstripe got his own place for a while, so he stopped playing in here.

I figured the brass bands would last about three years in here, and that's what happened. Basically, we're a small place. As the brass bands started to fill the place up, other clubs started seeing a market for them. That was in direct competition with us, especially on weekends. So some of the brass bands would prefer to play at Tipitina's—I never figured out why, because they got their gigs out of playing here, and they weren't being paid more at those other places. I guess they must have thought that the other clubs were more prestigious.

I really regret what happened, but as I phased the brass bands out, no one else was booking them either. You don't see the brass bands much today in clubs. The only one that's playing a lot is the Rebirth, and they've always kept the Tuesday night at the Maple Leaf. Le Bon Temps Roulé on Magazine Street sort of picked up where we left off. The young brass bands didn't know me and that I knew the older musicians. So they didn't understand that I had an alternative to presenting the brass bands.

Looking back on it, I enjoyed having those bands here. We never did profit much from it. When we started to phase them out, we had acquired a reputation for New Orleans music. Financially, we do a lot better now—smaller bands, bigger crowds, for the most part.

Several things contributed to stopping the brass bands. Ruddley Thibodeaux, leader of the Algiers, had a lot of problems within the band—illness and so forth, and his wife was ill. So he was having a hard time keeping the band together. The Soul Rebels changed their music totally—they went into a more hard rap style, which didn't really fit in with the audience that I have here. New Birth just sort of faded out and started playing mostly at the House of Blues or Tipitina's. Our main bands were Tremé, Soul Rebels, New Birth, Algiers, and Pinstripe. And Mahogany played here on Sundays for quite a while. Brice Miller came in and asked us for a gig—he used to play here with the Algiers and the Tremé.

Most of the brass bands now just play mainly at festivals, that sort of thing. I'm glad that they have that opportunity. But the Tremé Brass Band still plays here, and we occasionally play another brass band.

Benny Jones probably influenced the younger bands more than anybody, because he's always found a place for the younger musicians to play in his band. He makes no bones about it—he calls his band the Tremé because he uses the musicians from that neighborhood. Quite a few of the kids got their start with him.

Ruddley Thibodeaux, Trumpet

BORN: Algiers, Louisiana, 1948

Founder and leader of the Algiers Brass Band

Interviewed by Kevin Herridge in July 2002

My name is Ruddley Thibodeaux, leader of the Algiers Brass Band and one of the original members. I'm from 449 LeBoeuf Street, corner of LeBoeuf and Eliza. I just made fifty-four years old, and I've been in Algiers all my life.

Photo by Marcel Joly

Now, when we started the Algiers Brass Band was about July of '87. We kinda all got together back in the days when I was coming up, when everything was segregated. Behrman School, right there, was a white-only high school, and L. B. Landry was the only black high school on this side of the river. So that meant that almost all the black people that come up over here went to L. B. Landry school, which also happened to be from junior high to senior high, so you got a chance to know everyone.

So that's how most of the members got acquainted. A lot of us were in the high school band but not necessarily at the same time. Mr. Othello Batiste—who was a gospel singer—was actually one of the founders of the band, and Frank Hooper, who was the trumpet player, got together and organized the band. They thought it would be nice to have a brass band based right here in Algiers, whereas Algiers was no stranger to second lines and brass bands. They had second lines here, but they hadn't had a brass band since Red Allen's father, who was last heard of with a brass band around 1947 or '46, somewhere round there.

As a matter of fact, Red Allen's house in the 400 block of Newton Street is still in the family name. The reason I know that is because of my day job. See, being a musician in New Orleans, a lot of time you need a day job. I work for the city, and I work in housing. So therefore I have occasion to look up different records. I spend a lot of time in the Notar-

ial Archives, not necessarily researching history but just to see who owns what so we can get out and get them to get it fixed up. But nonetheless, that's Henry Allen's family house still over there. They were the last people to have a brass band before we started over here.

So I guess how it kinda started was when Mr. Batiste, who I was speaking of, and Frank Hooper got together, picking the people they wanted to get for the band. So since Frank had been in the high school band in Landry, he knew that some of the guys that had been in the band were still playing music professionally. But I wasn't too much into this kinda music. As a matter of fact, I didn't think too much of it—you know, I'm gonna tell you all the truth.

But when he called up, I said I knew all the guys and we'll give it a shot, you know. So we get together in July of '87 and picked a name, and somebody said it's gotta be Algiers Brass Band, as we're all from Algiers. So they did that, and we started practicing, and I got to be one of the leaders of the band. I wasn't too much into being a leader. I was just into music, but I wanted to offer my assistance to help the band musically, and so I was like a coleader, and we moved on from there. So we started practicing, and as we started practicing as a group, we probably knew about two songs: "Bourbon Street Parade" and "When the Saints Go Marching In."

That's all we knew when we started. I imagine that other people knew songs, but as a group that's all we knew. So we built on that and built up our repertoire, and things started to move rather fast. Like, we started in July—probably about in August. Let me go back, just briefly. I guess around the latter part of July, first part of August, we had like a debut. Blaine Kern, who had the Mardi Gras World over on the West Bank and who's interested in anything and everything from Algiers, became like one of our mentors, one of our sponsors, and he offered up the den for a press conference to announce the formation of the new band. So we came out and played and everything.

Anyway, we did that, and we were playing here and there. Sometime around the latter part of August (I think Blaine had something to do with that, too), on Royal Street they got a lot of antique shops, and they were having some kinda block party. So we got a chance to go up there and perform for some self-promotion, you know, so people would know all about us. We were playing on the steps of the Wildlife and Fisheries building, and so this man walked up to us and said, "Y'all sound good." I said, "Thank you." He say, "Y'all interested in going to Japan?" So I said, "Yeah," you know, "I'm interested." But now I was a bit skeptical in my mind because, keep in mind, I had been playing a long time but just hadn't been playing in the brass band genre. People tell you all kinds of things, but I knew better than to say, "No, I'm not interested." But I didn't think nothing was going to come of it, and lo and behold, about two weeks later I started getting some correspondence.

Now just to show you how being in the right place at the right time . . . you know, I guess it might have been fate. The man turned out to be Bob Leblanc, and he was in charge of tourism for the State of Louisiana. More than that, he was a former Algerene! So I said, "What made you pick us?" And he said, "Well, I just try to help the boys—y'all's from Algiers and I'm from Algiers." It was just as simple as that, and from then on we did a tour of Japan in October.

We worked hard. We practiced two or three times a week, but, you know, I guess when you're trying to do something and people know you're sincere, they volunteer to help you, you know, and so things started moving. The gentleman that owns the restaurant and catering service right on the corner of Valette and Homer—George Rainey—he was the vice president of Zulu. So that next year, he put us in the parade—sight unseen. So that was our first year in the Zulu parade, and we moved on from then.

I know you've heard of Mr. Danny Barker. Matter of fact, in that same year, 1988, we were over at WWOZ playing on the radio, promoting our first anniversary. We were also selling raffle tickets. What we were doing, we were having a parade and a big party at the Elks Hall, right over there on Elmira Street, which is a historic place in Algiers—lot of famous musicians and stuff have played over there. So that was like a fund-raiser, and we were getting people to come out and help us celebrate our anniversary. But also, we going to make some money, too, by selling raffle tickets and having a party.

So anyway, we were playing, probably something like "Didn't He Ramble" and a couple of things on the radio. After a while, this old man come in the radio station and he said, "I was riding in my car and I heard the music. I just had to come over. I was going home but I decided to come to the radio station." I didn't know him, so he introduced himself. This was Danny Barker and he congratulated us on the way we sounded, and from then on we had made a very important friend who helped us further our career. We didn't know it at the time.

So I guess after that we probably went on and had our anniversary and did different other little gigs. Just things you do, you know, on your way through. I got a call from Mr. Barker, could have been seven or eight months later. He said this guy was in town doing a documentary on brass bands and liked the way we sound—we sound more traditional than the Olympia, which was a great compliment 'cause the Olympia go way back. That was one of my goals for the band, to try get at least an equal footing with them or at least somewhere close.

So anyway, the guy, whose name was Sinclair Bourne, came out, and as things would have it, one of the younger, like, auxiliary members of the band, his grandmother had died, so we just playing the funeral 'cause he's a friend, you know. So this guy that Mr.

Ruddley Thibodeaux and Danny Barker

Photo by Marcel Joly

Barker had sent come out, and he asked would he have permission from them to come out and film it. And the guy put it on a documentary that they put on the National Geographic Explorer *series. So you know, all these things just happening, you know.*

From then on we did parades and, like, in New Orleans it's kinda nice, if you want work and you happen to be in a brass band, you always got elections! You got elections coming up now, you know what I'm saying? You playing for the politicians. You got parties, weddings, all kind of stuff. You always find something to do. We were doing things like that and we did more traveling. Went back to Japan again, and from then on we traveled all around, did a lot of things.

Now that was going on fifteen years ago. The band is still going on. There's a barbershop on Teche Street in the ten hundred block. We just call it Teche Street barbershop. But the gentleman's name is Joseph Smith. They call him "Toot" for short because his daddy was a musician and his name was "Toot," and he just inherited the nickname. Anyway, that was our headquarters, and that's where we practice and do everything. I had never been in a band this long continuously, and I'm beginning to see what happened with the Olympia and a lot of other long-standing organizations: that as time passes things change in your life and everybody else's life. So a couple of guys have resigned—you know, they had enough of the music—and about three or four people died.

Mr. Sutton, our alto player, who, when we started, he was in his sixties—Norbert Sutton—he had played with Shirley and Lee and a bunch of others back then in the fifties. He played with Tommy Ridgley and all of them. I had met Sutton over here because before the Algiers Brass Band, Sutton and I and another guy was in a band—name of Edgar Johnson—we had a little progressive jazz band. I didn't play trumpet in that. I played piano. Mr. Sutton took sick and died after we made the first trip to Japan. He lasted about a year, and he eventually died of pneumonia. Naturally we played at his funeral. He played alto saxophone. It turned out, like he was a spirit and an influence, 'cause you need somebody experienced and somebody kinda settled. He turned out to be one of my best right-hand men. Doing things we needed to do—I could call him for his experience and to mediate disputes sometimes, all kinda things like that. But, anyway, Mr. Sutton was the first person that died.

As I say, Mr. Othello Batiste, who wasn't a musician in the band, was actually the founder of the band, and he really helped us to get things together. He died and we played at his funeral.

Then, next, well, not too long ago, our original bass drummer, Donald Harrison—we all call him "Chauncey,"—he died.

And then I had another guy I was thinking about—he died about a week after Frankie Badell. 'Cause he was calling me up to find out when the funeral was 'cause he was gonna play. His name was Thaddeus Ford. Thaddeus had joined the band as a trumpet player. Thaddeus was a little younger than me, but he had gray hair like me, so I said, "OK, so I got somebody look like me gonna be in the band." Unfortunately, Frank died, then Thaddeus dies. That's some of the changes that went on in the band over the course of about fifteen years.

All of these things happen, but, you know, suffice it to say I still got it going on. Some of you are kind of familiar with the New Orleans music scene, and there's a fantastic little trumpet player by the name of Irwin Mayfield, plays with a band called Los Hombres Calientes, the "hot boys." I always tell him, I say, "I knew you was a hot boy!" Anyway, he came up in the band, him and his brother—they were about eleven. He's always been short, but being eleven he was even shorter, you know. Got some pictures of him playing at a funeral.

So that kinda helped perpetuate things and put some vitality back in things. Matter of fact, Irwin was in the band. He had started, but then after a while he went to NOCCA [New Orleans Center for Creative Arts], but then (I think when Frank Hooper moved) I got Irwin again. I asked his momma, "Can he come play with us again?" He was about sixteen, and he was probably a better trumpet player than me almost then. It was great!

I'd get him in the band, and he'd be playing, so I had to play more. I couldn't sit back, you know. This is a youngster with fire. So I gotta get on my horses and do it.

The band now is basically the same instrumentation. We play mostly two trumpets, tenor sax, clarinet, trombone and a rhythm section made up of tuba, bass drum, and snare drum. I also didn't mention that my son came through too. He plays trumpet. He plays with me sometimes. But I don't think he's probably cut out to be a musician, like for life, you know. To be a musician for life, that's gotta be part of your makeup, you know. I used to tell the guys in the band that I hope this keeps going on, but if it didn't, I would still be playing—playing what I was playing before.

We started out with a grand marshal; then we had some disputes, so we got another grand marshal. I'm telling you, you're dealing with a bunch of personalities—all kinds of things happening. Yeah, everybody was from Algiers. And that lasted awhile, and as it stands now, I don't have a regular grand marshal. From time to time there's people I use. Going back to the days when the band was newer, you'd be doing all kinda stuff. You'd be doing parades, and you mostly only need a grand marshal for a parade. If you plan a party or a wedding or something like that, you don't need him. I got someone I use from time to time. Unfortunately he's not from Algiers.

We don't have a regular gig—not anymore. We kinda got into the convention thing, so we do a lot of things for conventions 'cause this is a tourism city. You got a lot of companies—Blaine Kern and them, too, you know we do things for them. People come into town. The entertainment directors put together things for them to do that's "New Orleans." So they might all be at a hotel, and they going to eat down at Pat O'Brien's, say, for instance. So what they gonna do that's "New Orleans"? They have a parade. That's where we come in. Parade 'em down or parade 'em to the boat. Things like that, you know, so that comes in pretty nice. So, no, we don't play at no club—not regularly anymore.

We used to play at a place round the corner at Valette and Homer. There was this guy Rainey who was vice president of Zulu that got us that first parade. He does, like, lunch and stuff and catering, and we hooked something up there. We used to play there every Thursday night. When we went to Japan, we had a lot of friends, and this lady—we call her "Mama San," everybody call her "Mama San"—she's rich. So anyway, she came to New Orleans. She came to the United States, but you know, she passed through New Orleans. She looked us up where we were playing, right there at Rainey's. Got a whole tour bus—you know, the bigger ones with all her people in it. Parked right there by Rainey's and had them a good time while we played.

Matter of fact, I was trying to get "Toot" Smith to come here 'cause he actually remembers Old Man Allen. Toot is sixty-six. He's been around! He used to be here when his daddy used to play. His daddy knew some of those older guys—Mr. [Manuel] Manetta and all of them, you know. Matter of fact, Mr. Manetta was my neighbor; he lived just across the street. I knew he was a musician, but I had no idea of his stature in music history in New Orleans. All I knew was, you know, he had this little house on the side where he give lessons at, and every evening he be going on his gig and stuff. I wasn't too interested in this kind of music, but it was a funny thing: once I got into it I had to kinda study it, build up our repertoire and know what we was doing. The more I got into it, the more I liked it. I used to call him Mr. Manetta, but I didn't know he was that great person, you know. How you say . . . you can't see the forest for the trees? He was right there, you know.

He is the uncle of Placide and Gerald [and Justin] Adams. He lived right in the middle of the four hundred block of LeBoeuf, and I lived right on the corner of LeBoeuf and Eliza at number 449. Mr. Manetta lived in a double house, and right on the side of the house was a little building, like a little miniature house, like a doll's house. Actually, that was his studio, and that's where he would give lessons. I guess even after he died it stayed there awhile, but then his wife died (his wife lasted longer than him), and they didn't have any children. They had relatives like Gerald and Placide and them. This is the story. I wasn't there, but they was all people from the neighborhood. My understanding is that Mrs. Manetta left the money that she did have to another lady—a neighbor, a lady in the block—and I don't know how it went. I guess they must have sold the house, and the house kinda got into bad shape, and the little building was in even worse shape, and it got demolished by the city. Ironically, let me tell y'all something: that's the business that I'm in. That's part of what I do for the city. I'm not sure whether I had a hand in it or not, but I could have.

I had met George Lewis. As a matter of fact, when I was in high school I had a little taste of this music. We used to play in the American Legion Band, and the American Legion Band would sometimes play for, like, the Jolly Bunch over there in Carrollton. I'd never met Mr. Lewis over here—I met him over there. But still, being young and coming up, I didn't know what was going on. I didn't know who I was with.

I used to read about Red Allen, but that was before I was in the business, and then I didn't know that he was from right off of Newton Street. It's just funny how things go, you know. Things was happening, and you didn't know they were happening right under your nose.

Before I formed the Algiers Brass Band, I used to play rhythm and blues and straight-ahead jazz. As I mentioned, me and this guy Mr. Sutton, we were in a band. Like, trumpet is my major instrument, but I write music and I like to play the piano, so when I started playing all that kind of jazz, I was playing piano. We played Miles Davis, Charlie Parker, that kind of stuff.

Algiers Brass Band *Marcel Joly*

By the way, I still like stuff like that, it's just that I appreciate this too. Do I like that stuff better? I couldn't say that. I've had this discussion with people before. Everything that I liked before, I still like. But this is something new, I mean new to me. It was there already. But I got into it and started learning about what it was. So I think I like it as well, put it like that. I got into the revival sort of round the end of it.

But Mr. Barker was instrumental in reviving the brass band scene, and we happen to run into Mr. Barker at a good time, too. The youngsters, all they had coming up was rhythm and blues and stuff they heard on the radio. So people like the Dirty Dozen and the Rebirth, they'd play a new kind of stuff, and it started bringing in more people, and that kinda helped the revival too. Like, when we started the band, I was aware of all that stuff, but my position was, the stuff that they was playing, I had played already. I liked it but wasn't too interested in playing it in a brass band. I can still go back and play it if I want, but I had taken my model for the brass band, just like the Olympia. Later on I started getting records of the Young Tuxedo and the Eureka, and that was my models, you know.

It's a funny thing, but when people talk about stuff like that, like the Dirty Dozen and maybe the Rebirth playing all that kinda new stuff, if you really look at it—even some of the records I got here . . . back in the early fifties and late forties—well, one of the things they play is "Feel So Good," which I mentioned was Shirley and Lee, who Mr. Sut-

ton had played with. It was strictly rhythm and blues. Now, believe it or not, that wasn't an old song; that was a modern song. So people calling themselves purists and trying to say how jazz is traditional and how things go—things have always been evolving. They tried to nail Louis Armstrong down to the times of the Hot 5 and Hot 7, and Louis Armstrong didn't stay there. Pops moved on. He moved on and played other kind of stuff, too. I still like stuff like that, but I like other kinda stuff, too. To me, everything's got its place.

We were talking how some of these older musicians played and stuff like that, and I said, "I got a degree in music from college, and so I try not to play out of tune 'cause when you learn music and they teach classes for music, you can't make yourself play out of tune. I can't do stuff like that 'cause that's my makeup." That's my background, and I gotta be true to that. I don't play the music like somebody that was self-taught. Some of the things they were playing out of tune. I don't think that's a tribute.

The early bands I used to play with were just rhythm and blues. The most popular band? We had a band called the Soul Brass and had a fantastic singer named Sonny. We probably lasted a year or something. I guess we burned out. I used to play with a guy called Rocky Charles, and sometimes they do some of his stuff on WWOZ. Charles was actually who I started out with. Charles is my boy!

Actually, I started playing music professionally going down on a gig. It was Charles who I went out there with. Charles is from across the river although he lives over this side now. Matter of fact, I was out on a gig with Charles and Huey Smith and them in Meridian, Mississippi. My mom and them had to come back and get us 'cause we got stranded out there with no money. And I was in school! This is a true story!

I was in school in Xavier. I guess it might have been about my second year. You know, you're young and you listen to all these promises of fame and fortune. So we got there with Huey Smith and them—just a big-time gig. Now, we got a band concert and I'm a music major. Band concert is part of your grade, but I'm so wrapped up I'm not going to the concert, I'm going out here. So we got out there to Meridian, Mississippi, and time'll show you how things change. Like, some of these guys I hung around with, they weren't too good as businessmen. Which is one of the reasons, probably, the Algiers Brass Band is successful, because having been through that, I wasn't going through it again.

We got on the gig out there in Meridian, maybe two or three hours late. You can't do that. First of all it's not the thing to do, and from a practical standpoint, like, a logical standpoint, you got these people out here in the country. This is probably the only thing going on, and so everybody's looking forward to that. So if you don't get there early or at a reasonable time, after a while they gonna think you're not coming. And then when you don't come, the man ain't gonna pay you, and this is basically what happened. We got there a couple hours late—nobody in the place. Whether the man was telling a story or not, he said, "The people were here. They didn't see your instruments . . . didn't see nobody . . . they left."

Well, like I say, some of the guys taking care of business; I just wanted to play music right there. People get deposits and stuff. Now, when I get a deposit, that's not my money, that's the money for the band to put aside, probably to pay people, or if something go wrong wherever you at, get you back home or whatever. But not those guys! When they get the deposit they go party and spend up the money, and we go out there broke. Now the Sister's about to put me out of school 'cause I was going to Xavier University—it's a Catholic institution. I done missed the band concert and was about to flunk out of school. But where I been I ain't earned no money. Matter of fact, I'm gonna tell y'all, I think I actually earned about thirty-five cents. Now, musicians sometimes say cents, they be talking about dollars, but no, this was thirty-five pennies! There was me and my partner, who played trombone—our parents actually came out there to come get us. We must have been about eighteen. I didn't know it then, but that was good training!

There was a little place that we was playing at up on Nunez Street. I got some pictures of me and some Japanese guys playing over there. And then the building got in a bad shape. I had to recommend it for demolition. It's kind of ironic. It's kind of funny sometimes, but that's the way things go. Mr. Manetta's studio has probably been gone about ten years or so; I think when we first started the band it was still around.

The Mandalay Room on Newton Street? It was a bar. There was music there. What I know about is that when I was about eleventh or twelfth grade, I used to go there because I looked old for my age. I had no business in there. I had some older friends, and I'd hang out there. There wasn't no, like, music too much in there. There'd just be music on the jukebox, but then sometime after they had music there. Since we had the band, we used to play there on Friday nights, every Friday. The building is owned by Toot the barber. He bought the building when the owner died.

There used to be all kinds of entertainment going on at the Greystone League. I used to play there, and the Neville Brothers—anybody in New Orleans music—Professor Longhair, everybody, just about everybody! We called it the Greystone Voter's League, but it was just the Greystone back then.

The Hershey Bar? To me it was just incidental in the history of Algiers. It was a pretty big bar. It was on the corner of Newton and Whitney, but in the beginning it was a bowling alley, when I was a little kid. My cousins used to work there setting up pins before they had automatic pinsetters. Then they closed down for a long time. Then some guys opened it up and painted the whole building brown—hence the name, the Hershey Bar.

They'd have entertainment and stuff going on there, but it was just another bar to me.

Toot remembers when Ray Charles and people played at the Elks Hall. He went to see Ray Charles there. When I was coming up, they'd have dances and stuff in there. At first I guess I was a bit too young, and when I got older, there wasn't much going on there. Toot said Ray Charles cost about fifteen cents or something. I think one of the people Toot's dad played with was Kid Thomas Valentine.

I was the first musician in the family. My parents are actually from two little towns outside Lafayette—Grand Coteau and Sunset, Louisiana. I'm the first one the music bug bit. I was taught by William Houston and Earl Barron. Believe it or not, I used to sing, but I wanted to play the trumpet like Louis Armstrong. I really didn't know a whole lot about Louis Armstrong, but it was just the name was famous. So when I got into seventh grade, I really hadn't played music before. I guess it kind of mirrors the brass band. I wasn't into it that deep, but when I saw what it was about, I really got into it.

James "Little Twelve" Andrews, Trumpet

BORN: New Orleans, January 12, 1969

Played with Danny Barker's Roots of Jazz Brass Band; founder of the All Star Brass Band; currently with the New Birth Brass Band

Interviewed on the banks of the Mississippi River, November 2002

James Andrews and Mick Burns, November 2002

Photo by Emile Martyn

I was born in the Tremé as well as my brother Troy, a.k.a. Trombone Shorty. A couple of my uncles played with Fats Domino—they were Walter "Papoose" Nelson and Prince La La. My grandfather was Jesse Hill; he wrote the famous song "Oo Poo Pah Do." Then a couple of my cousins play with the Rebirth band, and a couple of them played with the Dirty Dozen. That's Revert Andrews and Glen Andrews. I have another brother named Terry Nelson; he plays snare drum with the Lil' Rascals Brass Band.

I came to playing music by being a kid in New Orleans. A long time ago, I used to be a tap dancer on Bourbon Street. I just had a wonderful love for music and watching all the old guys from the Preservation Hall and the Olympia Brass Band with Milton Batiste and Harold Dejan and the jazz funerals. I played a little bit in school, but I always wanted to play New Orleans brass band music because I love that sound. Milton Batiste was a childhood hero of mine—the Olympia was everywhere when I was a kid, the number one band.

Danny Barker came by my house one day. He was starting a band called Roots of Jazz with some kids my age. Some kind of way, I wound up playing the bass drum in that

band. I was around thirteen years old. Then we played at the World's Fair here in New Orleans in 1984, and after that I formed a band called the All Star Brass Band.

I was playing trumpet in that band. At that time, we had my brother Terry Nelson on snare drum, Kerwin James on tuba, Revert Andrews and Mark Jolly on trombones, and a guy called Larry Barabino. We used to play in Jackson Square. And there was Sammy Rimington Jr. on clarinet and Nicholas Payton on trumpet—he was about ten years old. We made some nice money, and when you play in Jackson Square, you get this feeling you're playing with different musicians passing through. After a while, you can go out in the world and play in front of any kind of crowd. It was a great experience. So Jackson Square was like a foundation that prepared you to go and play in any festival or any kind of club.

The way I learned the tunes was to go to Preservation Hall every night and listen at what they were doing. Or I would buy albums, take them home, and learn the tunes. It was just the regular traditional songs everybody was playing around town—"St. James Infirmary," "St. Louis Blues," "When You're Smiling," different things like that. That went on for a long time, around ten years. I started with brass bands because in the Tremé we always have second lines. I guess it was part of my nature, being from that neighborhood.

I became a musician because I love the music, and I love to perform in front of people—it's that thing you get from the crowd, that energy and adrenaline. People listen to your music, and they feel warm, and they kind of respect you. You can make them happy.

I got a lot of trumpet influences from New Orleans players: Milton Batiste, Teddy Riley, Jack Willis, Gregg Stafford, Leroy Jones, Kid Sheik, Percy Humphrey, Thomas Jefferson—he was one of the guys that influenced me most. I saw him at the Famous Door when I was a kid.

I used to see the respect that they got from being a bandleader, and how the guys looked up to them, how they worked together and knocked the songs off. Then, by being in festivals later on, I got introduced to people like Clark Terry and Dizzy Gillespie.

As a kid, I was in a social and pleasure club in the Tremé called the Money Wasters. They'd parade around the city and do jazz funerals when a member died. So the brass band thing was always somewhere close in my life, even up to today. A long time ago in Congo Square, they used to do a celebration on Louis Armstrong's birthday, the Fourth of July. They had something they called the Soundalike Contest. I didn't know what I was doing, but I've always had an ear—I could hear stuff and pick it up. I entered the contest a lot of times and didn't win for a lot of years. When we got it together with the All Star band, we came there and won the contest for a few years. We started to win in the early eighties. Then I got the chance to play with Clyde Kerr Sr. and the Young Tuxedo with Herman Sherman. I saw older guys like Clem Tervalon.

All Star Brass Band (Terry Nelson, Kerwin James, Mark Jolly, Sammy Rimington Jr., James Andrews)
Photo by Marcel Joly

The All Star band got booked overseas a lot. The first trip we did was to Milan, Italy, in the early eighties. After that, it all fell into place. We started getting offers to play on the SS Norway *cruise line floating jazz festival and in Arizona at the festival there. We were doing our own representation. Kids playing New Orleans music always goes over well.*

I toured with the Tremé Brass Band a lot and wrote a few songs for them; there was one called "Gimme My Money Back." It wasn't based on any personal experience, but it was a catchy title. In between times, I played in Jackson Square with Tuba Fats.

How Satchmo of the Ghetto *came about was some people used to call me that. Quincy Jones had heard me when he was down here, and he asked me if I would like to be the subject of a documentary. I said, "Why not? It couldn't do nothing but help." It was a good move—I got a lot of gigs out of it. I got to tour the world again, for real money this time. I put the music together in my head, and they had somebody with me that was writing it down as I was putting it on. The documentary was on TV all over the country. Then I got a call from Allen Toussaint, saying, "Would you like to do a CD?" It was all falling into place. Me, Allen Toussaint, and Dr. John went in the studio. I had about eight songs ready in my head—Allen wrote them down, and he came up with some stuff. It was a wonderful thing, man.*

It made a big difference to me. It gave me the chance to get out of the brass bands for a little while and into a more mainstream thing—concerts, stuff like that, where I was fronting a piano, drums, bass, and horn section—funk and rock 'n' roll. I started doing some nice gigs that paid thousands of dollars. I really wanted to do it.

I haven't got tired of brass bands, because you can never get enough of that stuff. Any time I hear a brass band, it just jumps, that adrenaline. Especially when the crowd is second lining—when you see them dancing, you know you got them, there's something happening. The band is just part of that energy. It's like a generator—the band kicks in the power, and then the people take it from there.

James Andrews *Photo by Peter Nissen*

It makes a difference whether you're playing in the Tremé or for a bunch of white college kids uptown. Because of the culture: when the band plays in the Tremé, it's a different feeling. You've got Congo Square there, and you got the people that are from that culture, and you got other people from around America and the rest of the world, and they're listening to the music. So I would say the groove is different. You get the college students, they're just drinking and talking and listening to the music. But in the Tremé, it's more of a culture thing. It's more satisfying, because that feeling and culture is worth more than anything to me. I'm very proud of all that, and I've had the chance to travel the world and share what I learned in the Tremé.

It's difficult to describe the Tremé. First of all, it's an American black neighborhood in New Orleans. Its present culture comes from a long time ago. The music is wonderful there; it's got its own flavor. Each neighborhood in New Orleans has its own flavor, the way it flows and the way the people flow. But you can go to the Tremé and catch a parade anytime—the character and the feeling that you get is different from anywhere else in town.

Who knows where the music will be in five years? I think the music will still be in the Tremé after we're gone. I think they'll be second lining in New Orleans for generations to come.

Lajoie "Butch" Gomez, Saxophones

BORN: New Orleans, April 12, 1946

Played with the Storyville Stompers and the Tremé Brass Band; founder and current leader of the Regal Brass Band

Interviewed at his home in Eden Isles, Louisiana, November 2002

My mother was a stage mother; my sisters used to dance. The family was very good friends with a number of the white Italian jazz musicians. Tony Almerico, Russ Papalia, Val Barbera, several of the older guys. On Sunday mornings, there was a radio show from the Old Parisian Room on Royal Street. Tony Almerico's band played, and the family would go over there. Sometimes I would sing with the band. I was about six years old at the time.

So I grew up in the music scene and started playing in grammar school, on clarinet. When I got to junior high school, I started my own rock and roll band, playing tenor. The band was called the Starlights. Mac Rebennack, better known as Dr. John, played in that band with us. His family was from across the river, from Westwego, and then they moved to the Third Ward. I don't know where he lived himself—you were lucky if he showed up.

I started playing with a band called the Storyville Stompers. There was a whole bunch of people from my school; some of them could play and some of them couldn't. The band started doing well, so the more serious people broke off and formed the Storyville Stompers; that was in the late sixties. Some of those guys are still there.

I wanted to play with some of the older people, so I quit the Stompers and started the Regal Brass Band. I put my dream band together. There was Alan Jaffe on bass horn, Kid Sheik on trumpet, Clem Tervalon on trombone, Benny Jones on bass drum, Gregg Stafford on trumpet, Boogie Breaux on snare, Chris Burke on clarinet, and Bill Shaeffer on tuba. I guess the Stompers just didn't have the feel; it wasn't the true music that I wanted to play. I went out and bought a copy of The Family Album *and started looking people up and contacting them.*

Then, from the brass band, I started doing a lot of sit-down jobs. I did a lot of work with Danny Barker, and when he couldn't make it, "Father" Al Lewis.

We rehearsed the Regal Band—we would sit round in a barroom in the Sixth Ward, drink a lot of beer, and play. The Regal didn't work much on the street; I first started getting jobs out of town. The older guys couldn't really travel much.

Our first real job was in Milan, Italy. It was a festival the day after Mardi Gras. Benny Jones and I got together—we were running the same band with two names. It was

the Regal when I booked the jobs and the Tremé when Benny booked them. His work was more local barrooms and social and pleasure clubs. I was trying to book festivals and concerts. For a long time, about two years, it was the same band. Then it got kind of ridiculous, so we decided to put all our eggs in one basket and go with the Tremé name.

Joe Jones, the singer who recorded "You Talk Too Much," lived in Los Angeles, and he was a distant cousin of Benny's. He had burned a lot of bridges behind him with New Orleans musicians. He bought a catalog of music, through a fluke, for a thousand dollars, went out to L.A.; it had people like the Dixie Cups, Tommy Ridgley, people like that. Joe Jones started promoting the music and not paying the artists.

He wasn't welcome in New Orleans for quite a while, so when the brass band thing started picking up, he wanted in on it; that was his way of trying to get back in. He created some problems between Benny Jones and me. I think he told Benny that I stole eighty thousand dollars from the band. We didn't make anywhere near that—I wish we had. I was the white devil, and I shouldn't be taking black musicians out of New Orleans and creating all these problems. Joe Jones stayed in Los Angeles—he had leased the Dixie Cups' version of "Iko Iko" for use in the movie Rain Man for quite a lot of money, but the Dixie Cups got nothing. That was his way of working.

Benny's a really nice man, and I think he just didn't know how to handle the problems. Joe Jones started calling everyone I did business with, telling them I was a crook, that he was representing the band, and that I couldn't take them anywhere. So I left and took Kenneth Terry, Kerwin James, and Keith Anderson with me. Revert Andrews had left the Tremé to go with the Dirty Dozen sometime in the eighties.

I played soprano sax, because I just don't like clarinet. I started learning more about Sidney Bechet—I played a lot of harmonies with the trumpet.

Almost the whole of the Tremé came with me into the Regal—it was Benny and Lionel Batiste who were left. Which was really sad. I loved the band, and I think it would have had a good future. I wish we could have stayed together.

The Tremé's still working, but I don't think they're realizing their full potential—on the other hand, I don't think Benny likes to travel a lot. And I don't think anyone's really handling the business for them.

The Regal's been around a long time. I guess our first job was in the early seventies. We're still working. I try to keep it traditional, even though we do a lot of the newer brass band stuff—Rebirth-type music. Keith Anderson and Kenneth Terry both played with the Rebirth, and Kerwin James is Philip Frazier's brother; they still like to do that, and so do I sometimes. We don't really rehearse. Most brass bands do the same songs, in the same keys, with basically the same arrangements, so everybody knows what's going

Regal Brass Band (Kerwin James, John Gilbert, Kerry Hunter, Keith Anderson, Tanio Hingle; seated: Kenneth Terry, Butch Gomez) *Courtesy Butch Gomez*

to happen. *I have a set drummer called Brian Lewis who works stage jobs with us—he's heavily into the funk thing; he has a studio here in New Orleans. I also have a female vocalist with me now—she's our grand marshal when we have to march.*

The reason we're trying to do more stage work is that if we go somewhere out of town, as a marching band, we're like the dog and pony show. It's like the main acts are on the stage, so we entertain the crowd by marching all around in the mud for two hours. Then run here and run there—they tend to try to overwork the brass bands. In New Orleans, you don't have that problem: you're a brass band, and you do what you're supposed to do. Even though a second line lasts four hours, it's different. You get motivated, because of the crowd; they put out so much energy, and you can key off that.

If you go to Ascona and they ask you to walk through the streets, and then walk through some different streets, it's just not the same. When they offered us a marching tour of McDonald's in Germany, I turned it down. You contract to do certain things, and they're always coming up with extra work—we would have ended up working eight hours a day.

I love going to Europe in the summer. I prefer working on stage if we're playing funk things or if our female vocalist is singing gospel songs. But audiences are different outside New Orleans. If you walk through the streets here playing, you get motivated; the crowd really pushes you. If you do the same thing in Tallahassee, Florida, it's nice, and the people appreciate it, but you just miss that feeling of enthusiasm, so you have to work harder to make up.

When the Dirty Dozen first started, a lot of people just weren't open for the change. The way I looked at it is, brass band music's still evolving. Brass band music was, and it is, and it's going to be. It was basically the music of the people, something they wanted to hear when they were celebrating.

I think reading holds a band back. For a short time, I was working with a tuba player called Dimitri Smith, who had Smitty D's Brass Band. He tries to have everything very polished and smooth, but that's not what the music is. The music is a couple of shots of Jack Daniels and go and play. If it's too precise, it's not our music.

I remember being on stage with the Olympia Brass Band in Milan. I went up to Harold Dejan and said, "Hey, Harold, you wanna tune up?" He looked at me and said, "I tuned up in 1958."

I took the Olympia snare drummer, Boogie Breaux, on a job with me. He wouldn't go anywhere without a bottle of gin, and he'd been drinking from it. We got stopped in a traffic jam on the Huey P. Long Bridge while a train crossed. You don't realize how much that bridge moves until you're sitting still. Boogie was getting really nauseous. So we went and did the job. He was playing OK, but he was completely drunk. Suddenly, in the middle of a song, the drums just stopped. I looked around, and there was Boogie walking off with some girl. Afterwards, we were eating in a restaurant, and Boogie said, "I don't feel good" and collapsed face down in his food. But that was Boogie.

Brass band musicians are a wild bunch—they're hard to control. The street funk that the Rebirth plays definitely isn't traditional—it might be in thirty years time.

"DJ" Davis Rogan, Radio Announcer

BORN: New Orleans, December 30, 1967

Host of the *Brass Band Jam* radio program on WWOZ, 1991–1999

Interviewed at 3621 Burgundy Street, November 2002

There were two periods in my life when I was influenced by brass bands. I grew up right by a Baptist cemetery, so I had the chance to see the joyous part of jazz funerals when I was a kid. When I was in the third grade, I switched schools to McDonough 15, where the music director was Walter Payton.

So I pretty much took traditional jazz for granted, and in high school I got into funk music and punk rock. I was a DJ at WTUL before I left New Orleans to go to college. The Dirty Dozen played benefits for McDonough 15 around 1980. And I'd seen the Rebirth playing on the corner of Iberville and Bourbon for tips in 1988.

By then, the Dozen had become a national touring act, so they were gone most of the time. The Rebirth was becoming the number one street band. The guys in that band were my friends and contemporaries, but the Dozen were on a different professional level. There was a feeling at the time that they would lose their edge, but the Rebirth wanted to remain "street" and always be available for second lines and functions.

In 1991, I went to David Freeman at WWOZ radio, and he cleared the idea of my doing a radio program called Brass Band Jam. *I started the show to celebrate the brass band movement, and I put the emphasis on the more modern bands. Some people complained about that.*

The Soul Rebels had gone out to stake their own territory, with the reggae and the hip-hop thing. Then Hollywood arrived. A guy named Ron Seidelberg from Hollywood Records came in and said, "I want a band that mixes rap and brass band." So he went and gave Coolbone a quarter of a million dollars to make a record. Historically, Coolbone was created with this guy from out of town having the concept of mixing these elements. He hired some people to rap for them. Coolbone was an offshoot of the Soul Rebels; Steve Johnson, the trombone-playing leader, and his brother Ronell, another trombone player, had both been in the Soul Rebels.

There really was a boom in the mid-nineties; it was a golden era for this new style of music. I'm wondering where we go from here. Nowadays, a lot of the bands sound the same—you take a pop tune, and you do it in brass band style. The big stylistic leap was taken by the Dirty Dozen. But where else can it possibly go?

Around 1994, there was this feeling that it was going to blow up on a national level, in media terms. People would come onto the radio station when I was doing the Brass Band Jam *program and say, "We want brass bands to be as big as rap." They had this hard funky street sound, more bass—it was happening to pop music all over America.*

There's so much doubling up of musicians; sometimes it's as if there's just one huge band. When things happen, like three of the Rebirth leaving to join the New Birth, the whole thing starts to become pretty indistinguishable.

A Note on Ernest "Doc" Paulin, Trumpet

BORN: Wallace, Louisiana, June 26, 1906

Provided constant work throughout the years to many young musicians

Doc Paulin moved to New Orleans in the same year he started to play the trumpet, 1922. He formed his first band in 1928 and continued to lead nonunion brass bands, mainly at uptown parades, for an incredible seventy years or so. Many well-known musicians worked for Doc Paulin in their younger days: Tuba Fats, Flo Anckle, Gregg Stafford, Michael White, and Big Al Carson among them. But as time went on and Doc's six sons were able to play well enough, the band became increasingly a family affair. Edgar Smith, tuba player, recalled, "Instead of paying us twenty dollars, Doc could pay his kids ten dollars and tell them to go to bed."

Doc Paulin, 2001
Photo by Brian Wood

Michael White, clarinet player, said of his early introduction to brass band music:

> When I first started playing, music in the brass bands was still all traditional, and you would have sometimes thousands of people following these parades for hours and hours. And there was such a tremendous spirit and sense of abandon in these parades, like you were being a part of more than just people parading and music. The only thing that I've seen that I would parallel it to is some of the things I've studied and read about in West Africa.
>
> Strangely enough, a friend of the family had given us a few records. The first traditional record I heard was the Young Tuxedo Brass Band, *Jazz Begins*. I started playing along with that, and that was my introduction to brass band music. I had a friend at school, Big Al Carson—he was playing tuba at that time with Doc Paulin. We used to talk

Curtis Mitchell (bass),
Michael White (clarinet)
Photo by Peter Nissen

about it at Xavier University, and I said, "Man, I'd like to do that kind of thing. Maybe you could talk to them and see if I could get into that."

The New Orleans Jazz and Heritage Festival came up. Doc Paulin's band was playing, and I met him there. I told him I was interested in playing. I gave him my phone number, and about two weeks later, he called me.

Doc Paulin's a great teacher, in the sense that he taught a lot of the musical, as well as the spiritual and professional values. A lot of guys saw him as just somebody who used to fuss all the time, and make you do stuff. They saw him just like a policeman-type character. For example, when you had a job with Doc, you didn't go to where the job was; you went to his house, and he would take you. He was guaranteeing punctuality. He demanded that, whether you were playing in the worst neighborhoods or parades on Canal Street, that you had clean and pressed clothes, black pants, clean white shirt, solid black tie (not polka-dot, not striped), white band cap, and clean shoes. He inspected you—if you weren't right, he might send you home.

You're going back to values of the music. I think for a lot of musicians (although there are a lot of examples to the contrary) playing was a way of getting people to pay attention to you—it was a step up. A lot of people were very proud to be musicians. How you dressed and how you conducted yourself reflected on you, as well as how you performed. To reflect high standards of professionalism, a lot of musicians insisted on strict uniformity.

On many jobs we went on, people would comment about how good the band looked, and that seemed to help business a lot. In pictures, bands that dressed alike just seemed to be more impressive than if they just dressed any kind of way, in different outfits. Doc Paulin inherited and passed along that ethic.

Doc Paulin's musical heritage lives on today in the New Wave Brass Band, which includes Aaron Paulin on bass drum, Phillip Paulin on trumpet, Scott and Dwayne Paulin on trombones, Ricky Paulin on clarinet, and Roddy Paulin on alto saxophone. The tuba player is Ronell Johnson, who's related to the family by marriage.

Oscar Washington, Snare Drum

BORN: New Orleans, October 12, 1957

Played with the Doc Paulin Brass Band and for many years with the Pinstripe Brass Band; founder and leader of the New Wave Brass Band

Interviewed at the GHB Foundation, French Market Place, October 2002

There's always been drummers in our family: my grandfather, Oscar Senior, was a drummer, and my father, Oscar Junior. Mostly they freelanced.

Photo by Barry Martyn

My uncle was a gospel drummer. That's where it started for me, when I was little. All the respect and accolades he got, that's what inspired me to start playing. He would let me get up and play in church. I wasn't any good, but my effort was there.

Before I took up drums, I had wanted to be a trumpet player. Why that was—my mother's girl-friend was also her hairdresser. I happened to go over with my mother to her house. Her name was Miss Rosalie. While my mother was having her hair done, they sent me to see "Pops," who lived in the same building. I went back there—I was kind of scared. The whole of his room was covered with photos of different bands and people he had played with. I was fascinated. I thought, "I'm in a differ-ent world right now." He asked, "Son, do you like music?" He grabbed his horn, played a few scales, and a little tune. And he started to show me how to blow a trumpet. I couldn't get a sound out of it. We talked a bit more; then my mother came to collect me. I found out later it was Punch Miller. That would be in the late sixties.

Percy Humphrey was my family's insurance man. When he came round, I asked him about music. He asked me what instrument I wanted to play, and I told him the drums. Next time he called he brought me a pair of sticks. I had those sticks for years, but even-tually they got broken.

In elementary school, I got involved in learning the basics and reading music. Then junior high school and high school marching bands, and finally I played marching music

173

Aaron, Ricky, and Roddy Paulin
Photo by Peter Nissen

with the Southern University band in Baton Rouge when I went to college. I played snare drum or bass drum or full drum set—I wanted to be versatile. Whenever there was a gig and they needed a drummer, I was the man for the job.

I got involved in playing drum set, for some years, in my family church, Faith in God Temple. Some of the greatest rhythm patterns come out of the church. Most drummers can attest to that—if you're a drummer and you have any kind of background in gospel music, you really have some seasoning.

As far as the brass band scene is concerned, I started after Southern University; we formed a little brass band. A couple of the guys were already experienced brass band musicians; they were Doc Paulin's sons. Ricky played clarinet, and Dwayne played trombone. Their father, Doc Paulin, was really the initiator for most of the guys in my age group.

You came under his tutelage—the Doc Paulin band was like the feeder school. A lot of people came from him. I owe him a lot of credit for getting my feet wet in the brass band world. He had three bands working—he was that big. The first band was the majority of the top players. Then in the second band, you had some good players that were trying to get in the first band, and then you had the third band—that was the hopefuls! I had to start back there, in the third band. But I wasn't there long. I was about twenty-three years old. I had promised myself I'd become some kind of professional musician. We didn't read music. If Doc wanted to do a song you didn't know, you would have to get with one of the sons—they would show you what you had to do. I started out on the bass drum with Doc. Then, when I moved up to the first band with Doc's sons, I played snare drum.

After a short tenure with Doc Paulin, I joined with some other musicians to form our own brass band, which was the Pinstripe. We got off to a hot start. We hit the street so hard and built the name so good for ourselves, we were the hottest band on the street at one time. There was only us, the Tremé Brass Band, the Dirty Dozen, and the Majestic. Most of the older bands were fading out.

    We came at that time when we still had a little strength—we were young, consuming everything. There wasn't that much money—you just about broke even, everybody got something. Not like now, when money is like top demand—you want a reputable brass band today, you got to pay money for it. We went through plenty of hard knocks, and the band had some great talent, but the rewards weren't there back then. Herb McCarver was on snare drum; he became the leader of Pinstripe. We had Mark Smith on tuba, Robert Harris on trombone, we called the alto player "Monk," Dwight Miller played tenor sax. Robert Reed on trumpet. We had some top-notch musicians who wanted to get in the band.

    We used to play for a mixed crowd at second lines. We didn't just go with the funky street-type music—older people don't relate to that. It may sound good, but it's the meaning that counts. I'm very aware of that: music has a meaning, it's a universal language. We tried to stick to playing the old traditional tunes that we still do now, because when you travel, when you go overseas, people relate to that music because that's what they know. The things that Louis Armstrong and Jelly Roll Morton did, those are the tunes that made jazz.

    Mainly we did second line parades, funerals, sometimes parties. You do a second line parade now, you're going to be making a hundred to a hundred and twenty dollars. We wanted to have it so that the same rate applied to each band. So we agreed between the bands that we wouldn't accept second line parades for less than one hundred dollars. With funerals—they involve second lines, you still have to walk, and when you cut the body loose and rave it up, it's a second line again. You might not be paid as much on a regular second line, but it should be comparable.

Pinstripe is still functioning, but I left the band in 1994. I've always wanted to be a bandleader—I felt I could do it. Most bandleaders are horn players; there's not many who are percussionists. And I think I had reached that stage where I had exhausted myself with the Pinstripe, and it was time to make a move. The other guys in the band said, "If anyone should break away and form their own band, it should be you. We'll support you all the way." Some of the Pinstripe members came with me. They also were at a kind of plateau—they'd been in the band a long time and they wanted some new energy, to do something a little bit different.

At first, we were the Mellow Fellows Brass Band, but we rushed into it too fast, and it sort of fell apart. I was talking to a friend of mine who's a musician, and I mentioned that all the good band names were already taken. He said to me, "Man, y'all should call yourselves the New Wave Brass Band." I thought, that's not a brass band name, but I gave it a try, and it stuck.

I work as a policeman for the French Market Corporation, and that's how we got our first gig. They had brass bands on weekends—they called it Music in the Market. At the time, Bridget Turner was in charge of booking the bands. She took a liking to us and became our manager and booking agent. In the band then we had George Johnson on trumpet—he had been in the Pinstripe, but he wanted to broaden his horizons. I played snare drum, Aaron Paulin on bass drum, Ricky Paulin on clarinet, Dwayne Paulin on trombone, Robert Harris on trombone, and Mark Smith on tuba.

There's one thing the older musicians respect highly if you are an up-and-coming brass band, and that is if you wear the traditional attire and show respect for your audience before they hear you play a note. That meant parade cap, hatband, white shirt, black tie, pants, and shoes. Both the Pinstripe and the New Wave dressed like that. For something like a second line, we had our band T-shirts, parade cap, black pants, and shoes.

We played mainly traditional tunes, but we would mix in street music. That was stuff you made up yourself that has a funky beat to it. The horn players play rhythm patterns and riffs, mainly transposed from rhythm and blues tunes. That's what the young generation are doing, and there's so many of them now. When I started out, most of those guys weren't even born.

Eventually, I got the chance to take the New Wave band to Ascona festival in Switzerland. I had always wanted to go and play overseas. Audiences there are different—they are very supportive, more so than they are at home. Over here, they can get to hear you anytime, but in Europe, they're much more attentive. I just love it when we go overseas—you get treated on a different level. They're so thirsty for the music, they'll sit and listen to you all night. Here, it's like a level down.

Brice Miller, Trumpet

BORN: New Orleans, April 13, 1974

Played with the Pinstripe Brass Band; founder and leader of the Mahogany Brass Band

Interviewed at 3621 Burgundy Street, October 2002

Brice Miller and
Morten Nilsen
(trumpets),
Copenhagen

Photo by Peter Nissen

*My dad was a musician. He's Dwight Miller Sr. He's a saxophone player; he plays
with the Pinstripe Brass Band. That's how I got my start. I was almost born into music,
because not only did he play with the brass band, he would play the juke joints as well.
At that time, we were living at 1705 Pauline Street, in the Ninth Ward. My daddy grew
up uptown, in the Calliope housing development. All the members of the Pinstripe came
from that area. They all went to Booker T. Washington School. Dad grew up in the midst
of the second line culture. Every Sunday, there'd be a second line parade up there. He
grew up in the epicenter of jazz.*

*I remember when I was a kid following my dad to the second line and looking up
at him as he played. That was cool. This was when I was about five years old, getting
stomped on by all the big dudes.*

*Our house was a musical house. My dad was the leader of various club bands—he
played with several of those groups—so there would always be musicians hanging out
at the house, rehearsing and so forth. We had a music room, and when they weren't
rehearsing, the room was filled with instruments. There was the drum set, there was the
piano, there was the big Hammond organ, saxophones, trumpets, trombones. All the cats
would leave their horns at our house. My brother and I would sit in the music room, and
we would bang, beat, blow whatever we got our hands on.*

That was my formal introduction to music—playing other people's instruments. I was a self-taught musician; that's how I got started. My dad sent my brother and I to Werlein's for piano lessons; that's when they were on Canal Street. We'd jump on the Desire bus and go down there.

I got interested in the trumpet because my dad was trying to find a way to include me in the music. I think I must have been around eight or nine when they dressed me in a suit, umbrella, and some sunglasses. I became like the grand marshal for the Pinstripe Brass Band. I was the guy that danced around with the umbrella. The strange thing is I was very shy—that's why I wore the sunglasses, so that nobody could see my eyes.

Like most kids, I was fascinated by the drums—it's the instrument that makes the most noise with the least requirement. I played snare drum in the elementary school band. I think my dad wanted me to be a trumpet player—it was the Satchmo thing: every man in New Orleans wants his son to play trumpet. He bought me a cornet; I still have it now. My friend Murphy Watson was studying trumpet, and every evening after school, he'd sit down and give me lessons: how to get a proper tone and how to make the notes and so forth.

And after that, I was hanging out with my dad and seeing musicians like Robert Harris, Tuba Fats, Benny Jones, Lionel Batiste, Gregg Stafford, Gregory Davis, all those cats. It was those guys that encouraged me to treat the music seriously—many of them have not received their due credit and exposure. From seventh grade, I started studying trumpet at Andrew J. Bell School, in the Seventh Ward. My band director there was Donald Richardson. Finally I went to St. Augustine High School. But I got much more informal training. As a kid, on Saturdays, I would go and play in Jackson Square with various small groups that didn't have names.

Then I began playing with the Olympia Kids band, which Milton Batiste had created after the Junior Olympia. Dimitri Smith, the tuba player, was in charge of that band. We rehearsed at Batiste's house; he would come and give us a sermon now and then—how we should learn the tradition and culture of the music and how important that New Orleans sound is. It was a great experience.

My main influence on trumpet was George Johnson with the Pinstripe. I used to ask my dad about him: why is he still in New Orleans, why is he not rich and famous, why does he play in a brass band? I really looked up to him. And Dwayne Burns gave me a few lessons when I was in high school. He had a particular demeanor about him, so cool and debonair. My first professional gig was with the Pinstripe—it's the first time I got a dollar. I think I must have been in the ninth grade—that was in 1987.

They allowed me to start my own band, the Junior Pinstripe brass band. The Olympia Kids had phased out when we went to high school. There was a lot of things taking place, businesswise, that weren't right—it wasn't fair.

The Mahogany started when I was in high school, in 1991. It grew out of the Junior Pin-stripe. Then we changed the name to the Jazzy Gentlemen Brass Band. Finally, we became the Mahogany. The reason for the name changes was that we had been getting a lot of work as the Junior Pinstripe, but people would be confusing us with the regular Pinstripe. The music was pretty much the same style, but we were a lot younger. Jazzy Gentlemen was all about being cool and mature, although we were so young. That was the ideology behind that.

We dealt with a guy that was doing management for us, and he went and incor-porated the name Jazzy Gentlemen. Then he started booking another band using that name. I was only twenty; I had never thought of registering it myself.

I did some research—I was at Xavier University at the time. I was taking African American history classes, and I came upon the term "mahogany"—strong dark wood; plus I liked the association with the old Mahogany Hall on Basin Street, with its red walls and big mirrors. When I formed the Mahogany Brass Band, we would play at Donna's Bar and Grill and other clubs.

I've always tried to do something different. We had a newsletter every month called The Mahoganist. *It would have little jokes, information about the band. I didn't real-ize it, but when I stopped doing it, I started getting calls asking what had happened to the next issue. We would just bring it to the gigs and give it away.*

Learning the history of the music, and the history and culture of the city, made me realize that people like Jelly Roll Morton and Louis Armstrong had opened doors, and this was important to me as a young black man. This jazz is something that was created out of the soil of New Orleans by the labor of black men of that time. It's the one thing that a black man in America can stand fast and say, "This is mine." I looked at that identity—in order to move into the future, you have to understand yesterday.

I tapped into the tradition, by listening to records, by attending social club events, by having the pleasure of meeting greats like Danny Barker and seeing him perform. I was playing around with other bands; one of the most influential was the Tremé Brass Band, with "Uncle" Benny and "Uncle" Lionel. I've never really associated with musicians of my own age group; it's always been the older guys. Even today, most people think I'm in my mid-thirties, but I just made twenty-eight.

At that time, there were all these young bands—the Rebirth, the New Birth, the Lil' Rascals. They were all playing head songs and popular songs. They were kind of doing the same thing that the Dirty Dozen had done earlier. The scary thing was every band was doing the same thing. The only way you could learn traditional brass band music was by listening to a much older band, the Olympia, or the Tremé, or the Algiers. But there were no young musicians playing traditional. I told my band, "This is the music that we need to learn." We had to do it in a way that would still be interesting to our peer group. And I had to sell it to my musicians. So I came up with what I call "traditional swing." We'd play stuff like "I Found a New Baby," "Exactly like You," "Ice Cream," "My Blue Heaven," but we'd add little rhythmic figures and swing aspects to them to make them more fun. From that point, it kind of took off, and to this day, we're the youngest traditional brass band in the city.

It's mainly the older people that hire us; the younger folk want to hear that urban stuff. Not that there's anything wrong with that kind of music. We incorporate a little bit of that into what we do.

It's just that I realized that if somebody didn't hold on to the traditional music, it was going to disappear. I've taken that upon myself on trumpet, Robert Harris on trombone, and Kirk Joseph on tuba. Ronell Johnson plays trombone with us too. Frederick Shepherd plays saxophone with us, and I have a younger saxophonist called Eron Williams. My snare drummer is my cousin, Ebria Keiffer. He also started in the Olympia Kids. On bass drum we have David Wallace. For a while I had another trumpet player by the name of Omari Thomas; he came from Alabama.

Sometimes I write down chords for the band, especially if it's a song they don't know. I've written several original compositions in the traditional idiom—if you heard them, you'd think they were old songs. But music is self-expression, and I always leave space for the musicians to do their thing—they have to play themselves. Every instrument has a role; the trumpet's role is to play that melody. The trombone's job is to give us the grounding that we need, and the saxophone gives us the color, fills in the gaps. The tuba doesn't just play the bottom of the chord: it has to give us rhythm. The drummers give us the New Orleans groove.

We play conventions, wedding receptions, clubs around town. We used to do the Sunday night at Donna's Bar and Grill—it gave us some exposure, kept the band tight, and kept our chops up. The whole social and pleasure scene has changed over the years, and we only do about three second line jobs each year. The whole society of the people participating in the second lines has got much younger—they're not looking for the traditional music anymore. They're looking for that shake, sweat, dance, and jump music. The Dirty Dozen brought their own identity, their energy, their rebellion. I respect that band so much.

When I say traditional, some people think we're trying to hold on to something that's gone, but that's not it. We're bringing our own identity to it. I've always been an individual; I play my own way. Musical education is important—not only am I a teacher, but I'm a music teacher. As a matter of fact, I'm the jazz studies coordinator for the school board.

This city isn't the best city to live in; it's not the most profitable city, it certainly isn't the safest, but the music has held me here.

Norman Dixon, New Orleans Jazz and Heritage Festival Coordinator

Interviewed at 3621 Burgundy Street, October 2002

I have been doing the coordination of brass bands and social and pleasure clubs for Jazz Festival for thirty-two years now.

When I started, it was 1972. That was the first time they had it at the Fairgrounds. It happened through Doc Paulin's band. He was playing at the Jazz Festival, and he intro-duced me to Quint Davis, because I'm chair-man of the board of the Young Men Olympian Junior Benevolent Association. We're not a social and pleasure club; we're a benevolent association. We did Jazz Fest at first with only two clubs: there was the Young Men Olympian and the Scene Boosters. They're the two oldest clubs out there. We take it in

Norman Dixon   *Photo by Barry Martyn*

turns to open. For two or three years, Doc Paulin was the only brass band they had.

Then the crowd started to get so large Quint Davis and I had a meeting and decided to have some of the other social and pleasure clubs out there. Quint asked me to coordi-nate it. Now, today, from starting thirty years ago with just two clubs, I have fifty-five out there. We have three parades a day. For the last three years, I've had the Indians on the ground with me—whatever tribes Quint's having on stage.

We started with the younger brass bands around ten years ago. The Dirty Dozen came out there. I had the Pinstripe, the Majestic with Flo, The New Wave Brass Band, the Original Thunderstorm (that's Eddie Bo Parish's band), the Lil' Stooges. I'll take them, and the Hot 8 Brass Band, and I'll put them up against the Rebirth any day of the week.

We got the Mahogany Brass Band, led by Brice Miller (he's my cousin). They were the original band for the Young Men Olympian. Then there's the New Birth band with Tanio. And the Storyville Stompers—that's a white band. The Chosen Few with Anthony Lacen. The Tremé with Benny Jones. Steve Johnson's Coolbone. The Pinettes, that's a girl band. Oh, man, they're good. And you got the Tornado Brass Band—that's Greg

Davis. There's still the Olympia, the Lil' Rascals, the Algiers. Altogether, I have seventeen bands to coordinate, but there's more than that.

I do it because it's like rheumatism or arthritis—it's in my bones. I been doing it so long. Right now, they're hooked on the funk thing, because that's what the kids like to dance to, but people our age are more for the traditional.

Anyhow, come down to the parade on Sunday. Get your walking shoes on—you're going to be walking for four hours. When you get out there Sunday, you can get anything you want to eat. Red beans, hot sausage—and a beer's only going to cost you a dollar. Smoked sausage sandwich, only three dollars. The police will be in line before you!

Epilogue: Second Line on Sunday

The leaders of the Social Aid and Pleasure Clubs, embodying local notions of respectability and order, become the people who are in control of the street and take hold of the public imagination. All those who join in the second-line parade can partake in this order, this joyous space of power, dignity, self-reliance, and freedom.

—HELEN REGIS, "Second Lines, Minstrelsy, and the Contested Landscapes of New Orleans Afro-Creole Festivals"

People here can't get jobs, and it's hard. So people need to come together, and work together. We want that. We want the communication and we want happiness between the brothers and the sisters.
—UNNAMED ZULU CLUB OFFICIAL, *Jazz Parades: Feet Don't Fail Me Now*

The hand-lettered notice painted on the side of the grocery store reads:

NO DRUGS

NO WEAPONS

NO LOITERING

NO SHOTGUNS

It's a bleak reminder of the negative aspects of urban life in the Sixth Ward. But the weather is fine, the barbecue smells good, and the crowd beginning to arrive at the street corner seems to be in a holiday mood. The Sudan Social and Pleasure Club (established 1984, proclaims their banner) is parading today at twelve noon—or sometime around then—after all, this *is* New Orleans.

Starting point is the Tremé community center, opposite Craig School, on the corner of St. Philip and Villere. Musicians arrive on foot or pick-up truck, in twos and threes, calling greetings across the street "Hey, Mr. Jones! Mr. Benny Jones!" "Hey, Tuba, where y'at?"

Two or three pickup trucks parked at the street junction already have barbecue cooking up in the back, with smells of charcoal, hot sausage, and pork chops to drive you crazy. On a couple of vacant lots, there are little white tents also selling barbecue. And you can get beer, cold from the bin full of ice, to wash it down.

As my companion, Anthony "Tuba Fats" Lacen, observes, "Everybody got a little hustle." We sit on the steps at the back of Joe's Cozy Corner, a block away, while musicians, club members, and potential second liners mill around the Tremé Center—it looks a bit aimless, but everything will probably get started soon.

Up comes a lady with a little hustle—she's selling small pumpkin pies from a basket. She spots us as likely customers, and it goes like this:

LADY: Hey baby, how about one of these pies? Made them myself, just this morning.

TUBA: Naw, can't eat them pies, ain't got the teeth.

LADY: Well, how about your friend? [indicating me]

TUBA: Naw, he's worse than me.

LADY: Well, how about buying one anyway, for a tip?

TUBA: Naw.

LADY: Well, *fuck* y'all!

We retire into Joe's Cozy Corner (headquarters of the Jolly Bunch Ladies, says a sign on the wall) for a cold Bud and a sociable reception from the mainly elderly customers, inspired by courteous and friendly curiosity. Then out of the semidarkness of the bar, into the glare of the street, and back to the St. Philip corner: maybe there's something happening by now.

There is. At the end of the walkway into the Tremé center, right by the entrance, Benny Jones and the Tremé Brass Band are playing the spiritual "I'll Fly Away." Benny's playing bass drum today and has a big band with him. There's Roger Lewis on alto sax, Elliott "Stackman" Callier on tenor. Mervyn "Kid Merv" Campbell and William Smith on trumpets, Charles Joseph and Eddie "Bo" Parish on trombones, and—surprise!—Kirk Joseph and Julius "Jap" McKee *and* Jeffrey Hills: three sousaphones in one band!

Already on the street, dancing in formation, is the children's division of the Sudan, maybe twenty of them, the boys wearing the same outfits as their fathers—and holding unlit cigars. According to Helen Regis, "The cigar-chewing six-year-old boy in the Sudan's youth division is not just learning to participate in community tradition: he signifies the club's (and no doubt his own parent's) hopes for the financial success of their youth."[31] As one club member noted in the TV documentary *Jazz Parades: Feet Don't Fail Me Now,* the social and pleasure clubs help keep kids out of serious trouble: "Some of these kids want so bad to be a part of that life. The parents will spend their last dime just so's a son or daughter can be involved in this. Some of the kids may get into a little trouble—they get into one of these clubs, they know that if they get into too much stuff, they can't belong. So that kind of keeps them straight."[32]

One by one, out of the center, down the walkway by the side of the police barrier, comes the membership of the Sudan Social and Pleasure Club. The crowd, by now a couple of hundred strong, gives each of them a big individual reception. And each of them responds with their best moves—this is *their* day; they've been saving and planning for it for months, and as they would say, "If you ain't gonna shake it, why did you bring it?"

Meanwhile, "Uncle" Lionel Batiste, super-dignified in black homburg and coat, unimpressed by the shenanigans and impatient to be away, starts leading the parade—on his own. The police escort get themselves together, the Tremé band falls into place at the head of the procession, followed by a division—about thirty or so—of the Sudan, a few hundred second liners form up, and the whole thing starts moving along Villere towards Ursuline.

The Sudan members look great—pale blue suits made out of some kind of satin material, white shirts, dark blue derby hats, white gloves. In the left hand, an unlit "big shot" cigar, and in the right hand, well, there may be a word for it, but I've no idea what it is. Imagine a walking stick, painted white, with most of the stick part enclosed in a sort of decorative box, made out of polystyrene, painted light and dark blue, and with glitter lettering—"Sudan" and "1984–2002." A sort of "walking box."

From time to time, the head of the procession stops to let the rest catch up. The walking boxes are rested on the ground, and the Sudan dance in the roadway—one of them is hit by cramp in both legs and falls to the ground laughing.

The Tremé is playing wonderfully, and the unconventional three-part bass horn section sounds great. The drummers have been joined by a tambourine player and a guy hitting a bottle with a drumstick. Although Benny's always very insistent that he sticks to the traditional music, it's a fairly loose interpretation of the traditional repertoire—after all, these second liners are from all age groups. By now, there are maybe a couple of thousand following the parade, and the energy and adrenaline are picking up.

The band plays "Hi Heel Sneakers," "When My Dreamboat Comes Home," "Blackbird Special," "Iko Iko," "Second Line," "Food Stamp Blues," and "Gimme My Money Back"—it has all the wildness and excitement I remember from the Olympia in the late eighties.

Hard on their heels, just behind the first division of the Sudan, comes the New Birth Brass Band, which includes leader Tanio Hingle on bass drum, his usual sidekick Kerry "Fatman" Hunter on snare and some other percussion including cowbell and tambourine, Kenneth Terry on trumpet, Kerwin James on sousaphone, and the incredible Frederick Shepherd (Fred Shep) on tenor saxophone, parade cap on backwards as usual, blowing his ass off, as usual. I don't know which band is better—they both sound fabulous to me.

Bringing up the rear is the Lil' Rascals, but I never dropped back far enough to hear them. The vibe from the crowd is sheer joy, the energy is as tangible as the electrical charge before a thunderstorm, and the mood is forward—to try and drop back down the line would be to defy the impetus.

One woman tries to go against the flow, and is rewarded by a chant from the crowd, "Mooove, bitch, git out the way! Mooove, bitch, git out the way! Mooove, bitch. . . ." So she does.

The barbecue vendors have kept pace with the parade, and so, incredibly, have the cold beer salesmen. Over on the neutral ground (what those outside New Orleans would call the "median"), a couple of operators are splitting cigars and adding herb to make "blunts." Soon, the sweet smell of skunk weed, protected by the sheer density of the crowd, winds up the euphoria another couple of notches.

By now the parade has been joined by around ten men on beautiful chestnut horses, riding western saddles—the Seventh Ward Cowboys.

The bands and the crowd, the music and the dancing, feed off each other—I don't know where else you could experience this sense of movement and purpose and elation.

There's about half an hour to go before the city permit runs out and the police disperse the crowd, when we pass Dooky Chase's restaurant. Hunger and fatigue strike like lightning, and the prospect of a seafood platter, a cold beer, a comfortable chair, and air conditioning is irresistible. So we go for it.

"It is only by plunging into the crowd that one can begin to apprehend the complex experiential reality of 'the line,'" writes Helen Regis.[33] In other words, you really had to be there.

Select Discography

The following recordings provide a good overview of the brass band movement's evolution over the last thirty years or so.

Leroy Jones and His Hurricane Marching Brass Band of New Orleans.
   Lo An. No catalog number. Recorded March 1975.

Dirty Dozen Brass Band. *Live: Mardi Gras in Montreux.*
   Rounder. ROUN2052. Recorded July 1985.

Tuba Fats' Chosen Few Brass Band. *Street Music.*
   Jazz Crusade. JCDD-3080. Recorded November 1985.

Rebirth Brass Band. *Rebirth Kickin' It Live! The Glass House.*
   Special Delivery. SPDCD 1040. Recorded April 1990.

Tremé Brass Band. *I Got a Big Fat Woman.*
   Sound of New Orleans. SONO 1029. Recorded July 1990.

Soul Rebels. *Let Your Mind Be Free.*
   Mardi Gras. MG 1020. Recorded May 1994.

New Birth Brass Band. *D-Boy.*
   NYNO Music. 9604-Z. Recorded November 1996.

Paulin Brothers Jazz Band. *The Tradition Continues.*
   Self-produced. Released 1996.

Notes

1. Quoted in Mick Burns, *The Great Olympia Band* (New Orleans: Jazzology, 2001), 212.

2. Louis Armstrong, *Louis Armstrong, In His Own Words,* ed. Thomas Brothers (New York: Oxford University Press, 1999), 27.

3. Quoted in Burns, *Great Olympia Band,* 213.

4. Tape-recorded interview, Tremé Oral History Project, Amistad Research Center, Tulane University.

5. Ibid.

6. Quoted in Helen A. Regis, "Second Lines, Minstrelsy, and the Contested Landscapes of New Orleans Afro-Creole Festivals," *Cultural Anthropology* 14, no. 4 (1999): 476.

7. Regis, "Second Lines," 474.

8. Tape-recorded interview, Tremé Oral History Project.

9. Quoted in Regis, "Second Lines," 483.

10. Regis, "Second Lines," 496.

11. Quoted in Association for Cultural Equity, *Jazz Parades: Feet Don't Fail Me Now,* videocassette, produced, directed, and written by Alan Lomax, American Patchwork—Song and Stories of America series, no. 101 (PBS, 1990; Vestapol Video, 1998).

12. Louisiana Writers' Project, *Gumbo Ya-Ya,* compiled by Lyle Saxon (1945; reprint, New Orleans: Pelican, 1987), 395.

13. Quoted in Jason Berry, Jonathan Foose, and Tad Jones, *Up from the Cradle of Jazz: New Orleans Music since World War II* (Athens: University of Georgia Press, 1986), 12.

14. Quoted in Burns, *Great Olympia Band,* 28.

15. Tony Scherman, *Backbeat: Earl Palmer's Story* (Washington, D.C.: Smithsonian Institution, 1999), 154.

16. Tape-recorded interview, Tremé Oral History Project.

17. Quoted in Burns, *Great Olympia Band.* 169.

18. Ibid., 105.

19. Ibid., 211.

20. Tape-recorded interview, Tremé Oral History Project.

21. Ibid.

22. Ibid.

23. Quoted in Burns, *Great Olympia Band,* 194.

24. Louisiana Writers' Project, *Gumbo Ya-Ya,* 11.

25. Tape-recorded interview, Tremé Oral History Project.

26. Quoted in William Russell, *Oh, Mister Jelly! A Jelly Roll Morton Scrapbook* (Copenhagen: Jazz Media ApS, 1999), 106.

27. Henry Glass, interview by Richard B. Allen, Hogan Jazz Archive, Tulane University.

28. Quoted in Scherman, *Backbeat,* 17.

29. Mac Rebennack (Dr. John) with John Rummel, *Under a Hoodoo Moon: The Life of Dr. John the Night Tripper* (New York: St. Martin's, 1994), 17–18.

30. Quoted in Burns, *Great Olympia Band,* 123.

31. Regis, "Second Lines," 488.

32. Quoted in Association for Cultural Equity, *Jazz Parades.*

33. Helen A. Regis, "Blackness and the Politics of Memory in the New Orleans Second Line," *American Ethnologist* 28, no. 4 (2001): 755.

Index